The Mystery Fancier

Volume 2 Number 1
January 1978

THE MYSTERY FANCIER

Volume 2 Number 1
January 1978

TABLE OF CONTENTS

```
MYSTERIOUSLY SPEAKING . . . . . . . . . . . . . . . . . . . . .  1
The Professorial Sleuth of Roy Winsor, by Larry L. French . . .  3
The Vengeance Novels of Brian Garfield, by George Kelley. . . .  5
Miscellaneous Mystery Mis-Mash, by Marvin Lachman  . . . . . . . 7
Chance and Illogic and The Black Box Murder, by E. F. Bleiler .  8
An Index of Books Reviewed in TMF Volume 1 (Including the Preview
    Issue), Compiled by Jeff Meyerson. . . . . . . . . . . . . . 9
The Nero Wolfe Saga, Part V, by Guy M. Townsend . . . . . . . . 15
THE LINE-UP (Fanzines and Such) . . . . . . . . . . . . . . . . 20
MYSTERY*FILE: Short Reviews by Steve Lewis. . . . . . . . . . . 21
VERDICTS (More Reviews) . . . . . . . . . . . . . . . . . . . . 31
THE DOCUMENTS IN THE CASE (Letters) . . . . . . . . . . . . . . 50
```

The MYSTERY FANcier
is edited and published by Guy M. Townsend,
1596 Hester Road, Memphis, TN 38116, USA.
Contributions of all descriptions welcomed.
Deadline for March issue: 1 February 1978.

Subscription rates: Domestic first class mail, $7.50 per year (6 issues); Overseas surface mail, $7.50; Overseas air mail, $12.00. Overseas subscribers please pay in international money order, check drawn on U.S. bank, or currency; no checks drawn on foreign banks, please. Make checks payable to Guy M. Townsend--I get some strange looks when I try to cash checks made out to "The Mystery Fancier".

The MYSTERY FANcier does run ads at reasonable rates ($5.00 for a full page and decreasing amounts for smaller ads). See the editorial comments regarding ads in one of the earlier numbers for a complete schedule (or write to me).

Copyright 1977 by Guy M. Townsend
All rights reserved for contributors.

MYSTERIOUSLY SPEAKING . . .

To state the obvious, I have returned. I did not stay in England as long as I intended (and I can't wait to go back again), but the press of other matters has delayed my putting out this issue even longer than my trip was to have done. But here it is, folks, and I hope you'll be happy with it. I forewarn you, though, that I put it together with even more than my usual haste, so typos no doubt abound. Also, I have done virtually no editing on this issue--I have typed directly from submitted manuscripts without taking time to alter misspellings or correct grammar or sentence structure (not that I go to great lengths to do this even when I do have time). And I have arbitrarily hyphenated words when I arrived at the right hand margin, with no great regard as to whether they are properly divided. In short, this is a rather sloppy issue, but it's got lots of good stuff in it. And these editorial comments are strictly off the cuff, prepared in desperate haste to get this thing together and in the mail before the end of the year, when all the copyright forms change and the rates go up.

At last we have some new cover art, and a super cover it is. I hope Al Fick will be good enough to do more of them for TMF. Not only is he one of the best artists in our midsts, he appears to be the *only* one.

I confess to being a bit disappointed at the number of subscription renewals. *AND BY THE WAY--YOU ARE ALL REMINDED TO SEND ME YOUR CHECKS AS SOON AS YOU GET THIS ISSUE.* I'm going to be optimistic and assume that most of those who did not resubscribe simply forgot to do so, and I'm sending TMF 2:1 to all who subscribed to volume one. This is going to be quite costly unless a good many of the delinquents do see the light and re-up.

On the subject of subscriptions, I have taken the perhaps misguided step of placing ads in the February (I think) issues of EQMM and AHMM. It will be interesting to see if there are many proto-fans out there just waiting to be identified.

I am very disappointed that this issue does not have a report on the '77 Bouchercon. Surely there were dozens of you folks at the gathering, and it is beyond me to understand why not a one of you sent an account of the activities to TMF. I know, I know--*I'd* rather be published in TAD, too, but TAD can only run one article--or at best a couple--on the subject, and TMF and its readers are eager for such news. How about something for the next issue? It wouldn't fall into the "not news" category in March, but I'm sure we'll all still be interested.

In the Preview Issue I declared that "The Line-Up" would be a feature in each number, but its relatively unchanging nature--coupled with the fact that all subscribers to volume one of TMF received the first issue of that volume, in which "The Line-Up" did appear--led me to opt in favor of making it an annual matter, appearing only in the first number of each volume. So here it is, folks; you won't see it again until next year. Should any bright new stars appear in the meantime I'll try to mention them in "Mysteriously Speaking . . .".

Speaking of "The Line-Up", I ran out of room on that page before I got to where I wanted to say a few things about DAPA-EM, so I'll say them here. DAPA-EM is *the* mystery amateur publication association. Its members all produce "apazines" of their own (from 1-2 pages to 30 pages and more), which are mailed to the association's editor who sorts them into packages containing one copy of each apazine and then mails these packages to each member of the association. The cost of membership is more or less limited to the cost of putting ones own apazine together. Sample mailings can be had from the editor (of DAPA-EM, that is) for $1.00. DAPA-EM is now taking a limited number of subscriptions from non-participants. The cost is $2.50 per mailing. DAPA-EM is bi-monthly, and its editor is Art Scott, 1089 Tanland Dr. #103, Palo Alto, CA 94303.

Most of us have articles "in us", so to speak; the problem is simply that of identifying the topics and motivating ourselves to get to work putting our ideas on paper. Articles for TMF need not be scholarly --indeed, they make for better reading if they are not scholarly. They need only be interesting (and moderately literate). Perhaps if we all throw out ideas about the kinds of articles we would like to read, it will draw the attention of some of us to an article or two we would like to write. Jeff Banks did something like this in a letter last year (though his suggestions were mainly for large scale projects), and I am hereby inviting all of TMF's readers to send in ideas about articles they would like to see in these pages.

Reviews we have in plenty, and I certainly don't want to discourage any contributors, but might I suggest that some of the energy now being expended on reviews be directed toward articles? An article really isn't much more difficult to write than a bunch of reviews. Besides, if you write an article your name gets much more prominent display on the contents page than it does with a review, or even several reviews. (In fact, this time I didn't have room to list all the individual items being reviewed, so the reviewers' names do not appear on the contents page at all.) And articles give one much more latitude for being opinionated (I speak from experience). So how about it? Surely there's someone out there just itching to throw rocks (or roses) at some author or some series, or express some cosmically profound ideas (in deathless prose) about some aspect of our noble genre. Here's your chance; all I ask is that you keep it clean (and literate).

Lastly (unless something else comes to mind before I jerk this sheet from the typewriter), I want to wish you all a Happy New Year and send you belated Seasons Greetings. I gave up sending cards many years ago (I think it was the year after I spent vast sums of money buying snazzy cards and the stamps to go with them, and spent hours addressing them, and then, as I discovered about the following July, forgot to mail the bloody things--AARRGH!), but I, no doubt presumptuously, think of you all as my friends, though I've never met most of you and probably never will, and it's the time of year for friends of whatever faith (or lack of same) to acknowledge their friendships, and since I'm the editor of this publication I'm taking this opportunity to do it on the cheap. If I could manage it, I'd give each of you a lifetime subscription to TAD, an Edgar for your first novel, and a chance to kick Newgate Calendar in the fanny. As it is, though, you'll just have to settle for my Best Wishes.

THE PROFESSORIAL SLEUTH OF ROY WINSOR
By Larry L. French

    I sat but a few steps from the celebrated oversized round table, which was positioned adjacent to the semi-circular bar. In the grill, a row of picture windows framed the tennis courts and the seventeenth fairway of the Pelham Country Club, and my host, with his balding head, casual dress and Ben Franklin glasses, perhaps resembled the "distinguished former professor of English at Brown", who had ventured about in Nantucket and herein, solving puzzles and glorifying the "art of detection."

    Roy Winsor, creator of Professor Ira Cobb is a most hospitable gentleman, a gifted writer, and winner of an "Edgar" by Mystery Writers of America for his first Ira Cobb Mystery, *The Corpse That Walked* (Fawcett, 1974). Although relatively new to the my stery game, Winsor has to his credit over twenty years of creative writing experience, mostly in the television-radio-advertising media: "Writing fiction is a new field for me and I enjoy its demands and its subjective rewards. I hope to continue to write this kind of book indefinitely." Winsor created three of the most notable "soap operas" ever to grace the TV screen, i.e., *Search for Tomorrow, Love of Life,* and *The Secret Storm*. In more recent years, Winsor operated his own production agency until deciding to "try his hand" at mystery writing. After *Corpse* have followed two more "Ira Cobb" mysteries, *Three Motives in Murder* (1976) and *Always Lock Your Bedroom Door* (1976).

    Subsequently, disaster struck, as Winsor's publisher (Fawcett) was purchased by CBS and the first order of the day was "no more mysteries." The problem is an acute one, as was noted in a recent issue of MWA's "Third Degree". Consequently, Winsor's fourth Cobb adventure, *A Sweet Way to Die,* has gone unpublished to date, and work on a fifth has been temporarily suspended.

    The interesting and favorable aspect of Roy Winsor is that he writes in the tradition of the "Golden Age", although his setting is modern and his methods American. He admits that his writings have been adequately influence by such notables as Conan Doyle, Christie and Carr and he is quick to express his dislike for the hard-boiled knights errant in Ross and John MacDonald, but considers them gifted imagists.

    Cobb is a return to the Golden Age detective, a college English professor who solves crimes as a hobby.

    Fred Dueren indicates in his "paperback crimes" (TAD 9/4) that "he is a blend of Asey Mayo's style, Nero Wolfe/Archie Goodwin's repartees, and Lew Archer's history-centered plots--all on a modest, less eccentric plane."

    The character Cobb is based upon an eccentric college professor that Winsor knew at Harvard College.

    The Sherlockian structure is present as Cobb is ably assisted by his own "Boswell", Dr. Steve Barnes, a Ph.D. himself, who marries one of the main characters in *Motives*. It is also noteworthy to mention that Cobb himself is a my stery writer, under the pen names of "A. S. Howland" and "Dr. Oscuro", which exists as his primary means of support for the early retired professor with a specialty in Jonathan Swift. A disaster of an early marriage has made him a confirmed bachelor with a kindly old Nantucket housekeeper (mrs. Pellagrin) in service (again, shades of S.H.). Cobb loves his "beef 'n ale", and is rather blustery in his own manner, a character reminiscent of John Dickson Carr's Gideon

Fell and perhaps even Stout's Nero Wolfe. He is described as "tall... almost gaunt, Lincolnesque, with thick, dark hair, bristling eyebrows and piercing brown eyes." Winsor notes that Cobb is "ruggedly handsome" and a "young" forty-eight years of age.

In *Motives*, Cobb is trying to unravel the murder of Ned Penrose, son of wealthy friends. Ned owed extensive gambling debts, got girls into several kinds of trouble, possibly tried to kill his mother and generally made himself a likely victim. *Motives* is strongest on plot and puzzle and a must for the traditionalist.

In *Bedroom* Cobb is again challenged by murder on the quaint New England island of Nantucket. Old Addie Hill, rich, envied and very frightened, summons Cobb to witness her new will. This will cuts out her younger husband and most of her greedy relatives who have been waiting impatiently for her to shuffle off this mortal coil. Suddenly, someone can no longer wait for Addie to die naturally.

The first Cobb adventure, *Corpse*, deals with a most incredible phenomenon--a corpse apparently moving itself which is only the beginning of an epidemic of murder and violence. Cobb comments:

"I'm not a professional sleuth. . . . But I do have rather remarkable research credits, and I've learned over the years that by asking questions, snooping if you will, and questioning the answers, discrepancies quite often show up."

With only a few clues, a merciless instinct and a nip of sherry now and then, Cobb sets about tracking down the murderer who was terrorizing the peaceful island of Nantucket.

A graduate of Harvard, who makes his home in beautiful and historic Pelham Manor, New York, Winsor recalls his reaction upon receiving the "Edgar":

"The weather was miserable that particular night and obviously we would not have gone to the city except for my nomination. There were five nominees for the "Edgar". Runners-up received scrolls. After four had been awarded I realized that my name had yet to be called and that there was no one else left to receive the Edgar except me!"

Upon his late return to Pelham Manor, Winsor suddenly had the possessed desire to "tell the world". After telephone calls to his daughters, all of whom were sleepy-eyed and generally unexcited, he and his wife ventured to the Club, where perhaps appropriately, in the midst of the "world of Ira Cobb", the Winsors celebrated with a few close friends, the "Edgar" standing proud on the semi-circular bar, being specifically admired by the Club waiter who later appeared in a second book.

Winsor has a special knack of telling a story which not only perpetrates a puzzle constituting a challenge to amateur sleuth Cobb, but creates an atmosphere quality, reminiscent of Carr and Christie, and boils down to what the layman would describe as pure entertainment.

Winsor himself is quite satisfied with his creation and so he should be. Assuming his publisher problems will be resolved, readers can look forward to many more adventures of Professor Cobb. After all, Sherlock, Hercule, Nero and Gideon (and of course H. M.) are all gone now, and "EQ" is tied up with EQMM. We have some excellent hard-boiled writers working, i.e., Parker, Bandy and McDonald, but the Roy Winsors are rare indeed. For a lack of publisher to extinguish one glimpse of hope for golden age detective fans, it would surely be a *crime!*

THE VENGEANCE NOVELS OF BRIAN GARFIELD
By George Kelley

It was sometime in 1974, the summer maybe. I went to see Charles Bronson in *Death Wish*. It wasn't so much the impact of the movie that startled me; rather, it was the impact of the audience.

Death Wish (Fawcett, 1972, 1974) was modified in the transition to a movie, but the essence remains: Paul Benjamin, middle-aged liberal, life-long citizen of New York City, has terror strike deep into his life.

During a robbery Benjamin's wife and daughter are savagely beaten by a trio of junkies.

Benjamin's wife dies, his daughter is reduced to a human vegetable.

And Benjamin? Well, we have all the makings of an Executioner vengeance trip, don't we? Benjamin doesn't let us down. He gets a pistol and lurks the streets and parks at night, offering himself as bait. It works. In a variety of settings, Benjamin wastes muggers, junkies, and other denizens of the underworld.

And, of course, the people love it. Benjamin is known as the Vigilante and hailed by the people of ravaged New York. And, during the movie, every time Bronson as Benjamin blew away a black mugger or a Rican junkie, the crowd went wild. They loved it, cheering and screaming for more.

You can hear the argument in any blue collar bar: killing is the only thing muggers and junkies understand; we should just kill them all!

In fact, in *Death Sentence* (Fawcett, 1975, 1976) Garfield has Paul Benjamin enter a bar and listen to those same arguments. And Benjamin, converted from his previous naive liberalism, agrees. He hits the streets of New York and before the end of *Death Wish* over a dozen "vermin" are dead. And the people and the police call the Vigilante a hero.

Benjamin's daughter, the vegetable, dies.

Afterwards, Benjamin decides it's time to move on. He transfers to Chicago in *Death Sentence* and guess what?

There are muggers and junkies in Chicago, too!

Well, you know what happens. Another killing spree. But, midway through the book, complications arise. Inspired by Benjamin's methods, another Vigilante takes to the streets. The death count of the "vermin" hits twenty-five. Some innocent people are gunned down by the other Vigilante. A close friend of Benjamin begins to suspect that Paul is the Vigilante.

Read together, *Death Wish* and *Death Sentence* remind me of the problem the producers of Clint Eastwood's "Dirty Harry" series had after they were criticized for the fascist first film, *Dirty Harry*. Clint, as a San Francisco police Inspector, wipes out lots of Bad Guys with his awesome .44 Magnum. The movie critics shouted that Dirty Harry was a dangerous maniac. So in the second Dirty Harry movie, *Magnum Force*, a group of fascist police officers decide to save the people the cost of trials and kill pimps, junkies, gangsters, etc.

Dirty Harry wipes out these Vigilantes, priving, I suppose, that he is indeed for due process.

But for other people.

The Garfield books are in the same dilemma. Once every man and woman become their own prosecutor, judge and jury, there is no law, only anarchy. Your neighbor then has a perfect right to blow your head off when your dog shits on his lawn. According to his law, your dog's offense is punishable by your death. Makes perfect sense.

The legal system is not supposed to be perfect. The best we can expect it to be is fair: promising us equal protection under the law. And, for all the criticism our system of justice has received, it works. It's slow, cumbersome, imperfect, but it works. I'd rather be tried in the United States for any crim I'm accused of than in any other country in the world.

Which brings us to Garfield's latest book, *Recoil* (Morrow, 1977). Where *Death Wish* and *Death Sentence* were, at best, a slick reworking of the Executioner genre, *Recoil* offers us something more sophisticated.

The plot is interesting. Fred Mathieson's testimony puts gangster Frank Pastor behind bars for eight years. Pastor gets out and wants the people who testified against him killed.

The wrinkle is that the government relocated the witnesses after the trial, giving them new identities and new lives. But Pastor is adamant; honor is at stake here. The witnesses must be killed. And, of course, Pastor discovers their identities and sets out to kill them.

Fred Mathieson and his family narrowly escape death by Pastor's hit men; immediately they go underground.

But Mathieson is tired of the worry, the threat that Pastor presents. He decides to counterattack.

Mathieson hires a charismatic private detective to train him in methods of fighting Pastor.

But, the important factor is, Mathieson doesn't want to kill Pastor or anyone else!

This is a radical departure from the two previous books; here Garfield is exploring the notion of vengeance without death.

And, surprisingly enough, he pulls it off.

Recoil, Though just a bit unrealistic in parts, is a solid thoughtful piece of work and deserves readers. The suspense is rivetting and the plot is tight.

Death Wish and *Death Sentence* are forgettable, but *Recoil* is first-class Garfield and I urge you to read it.

MISCELLANEOUS MYSTERY MISH-MASH
By Marvin Lachman

Mystery writers of the early 1940's were oddly prophetic in anticipating the society of a quarter of a century later. In *The Weak-Eyed Bat* (1942), Margaret Millar confronts her psychiatrist-detective, Paul Prye, with a particularly obnoxious 18 year old who seems to hate all adults. In reaction to her diatribes, Prye asks her, "Could there be a new Youth Movement for the suppression of everyone over 30?" It was in 1943, with his *Dead on the Track*, that John Rhode gave the following unisex description: "So many chaps wore their hair curled these days. And with so many women wearing trousers it was difficult to tell them apart, short of undressing them." The following year, Helen McCloy in *Panic* gave the following ecologically sound description from the vantage point of a remote cabin in the Adirondacks: "In a city you thought of all life as human life. You had to live in the heart of the woods to realize that humanity was a slight ripple on the surface of a flood of life that seeped into every vacant crack, flowed into every biological vacuum the moment it occurred. . . . You couldn't turn around without running into some form of life tortured into countless fantastic shapes by the agony of adaptation, all urgent, devouring, tireless--silently disputing man's assumption that the earth was created for his convenience alone."

Mystery writers love "in jokes". In John Evans' *Halo in Blood* (1946), a client comments on the allegedly odd reading tastes of Private Eye Paul Pine, pointing, among other books, to a book by Howard Browne (John Evans is a pseudonym of Howard Browne.) Brandon Bird dedicated his mystery *Death in Four Colors* (1950): "To Kay and George, without whom this book would have been impossible." It certainly would have been impossible since "Brandon Bird" is the pseudonym of Kay and George Evans.

It was probably not a coincidence that Dr. Doris Ball, in choosing a pseudonym for her second career, as a mystery writer, selected "Josephine Bell", the female version of the name of the real-life doctor upon whom Doyle patterned Sherlock Holmes. Nor do I think it was an accident that George Goodchild in *Death on the Centre Court* (1935) gave one character, a church official, the last name of Blake, thus making him Sexton Blake.

If one seeks, there are detectives for every day of the week, namely:

WEEKDAY	DETECTIVE	CREATOR	TITLE
Sunday	Aunt Sunday	Joseph Farjeon	*Aunt Sunday Sees It Through* (1940); U.S. title: *Aunt Sunday Takes Command*
Monday	Todd Mundy (ouch!)	Brook Hastings	*The Demon Within* (1953)
Tuesday	The Tuesday Club (featuring Miss Marple)	Agatha Christie	*The 13 Problems* (1953) U.S. title: *The Tuesday Club Murders*
Wednesday	Aunt Wednesday	Joseph Farjeon	Same as for Sunday
Thursday	Max Thursday	Wade Miller	*Guilty Bystander* (1947)
Friday	Joe Friday	Richard Deming	*Dragnet: The Case of the Courteous Killer* (1958)
Saturday	Johnny Saturday	Lawrence Goldman	*Fall Guy for Murder* (1943)

CHANCE AND ILLOGIC AND THE BLACK BOX MURDER
By E. F. Bleiler

The Black Box Murder by the Anglo-Dutch author Maarten Maartens is one of the almost legendary rarities of detective fiction. Howard Haycraft mentioned it in passing in *Murder for Pleasure*, and had read it; but Barzun and Taylor, and Glover and Greene do not list it in their collections. The New York Public Library and the Mercantile Library, which are excellent on obscure turn-of-the-century fiction, do not own copies. And, years ago, when I lived in Chicago, Vince Starrett once gave me a list of impossible books he had long been trying to find: *Zambra the Detective, The Divinations of Kala Persad, A.B.C. Investigates* and *The Black Box Murder*. I eventually found the first three for him, but never even had a smell of Maartens.

A couple of months ago while I was working on the introduction to *The Passenger from Scotland Yard* by Harry Freeman Wood, I advertised for additional copies of *The Passenger* to check editions for reproduction. In one ad, by chance, I listed only the title of the book, and forgot to add Wood's name. A little while later I got a quote in the mail, offering *The Passenger*. But when the book came in I was shocked to see that it was attributed to one William Ward, although the text was Wood's. The Publisher was Westbrook of Cleveland.

The Shock came from the fact that Wood is a very mysterious person, and I had a lot of trouble finding out very little about him. And now the question of authorship seemed to be thrown open again. I went straight to the reference books and started checking. I discovered that not only was there an edition of *The Passenger* attributed to Ward, but that there were several other books under this name: several Jesse James stories, and a book called *The Black Box Murder*. All were paperbacks published by a dime-novel publisher, Arthur Westbrook of Cleveland. They were undated, but probably printed some time in the early 1920's.

The situation was then obvious. "William Ward" was a house name, put onto old books by an unscrupulous publisher to gain new sales.

Illogic then entered. If *The Passenger* had been stolen from Wood, *The Black Box Murder* was probably stolen from Maartens.

I managed to turn up a copy of the Westbrook edition of *The Black Box Murder*, and lo, in this case, William Ward equals Maarten Maartens. Westbrook obviously took an earlier American edition (probably the American Book Company plates) and used very worn stereo plates, altering the title page.

On checking further I discovered that *The Black Box Murder* has apparently never been published under Maarten's name. The original British edition (Remington, 1889) was attributed to "The Man Who Discovered the Murderer." Pirated American editions copied this authorship, which counts as anonymous publication, and then Westbrook finished it off with William Ward. This hidden authorship is probably one of the reasons that this novel has been so hard to find. We have all been looking for it under the wrong authorship.

AN INDEX OF BOOKS REVIEWED IN TMF VOLUME I
(Including the Preview Issue)
Compiled by Jeff Meyerson

Author, TITLE   (Reviewer) Issue:Page

Aarons, E. S., ASSIGNMENT--AFGHAN DRAGON (Steve Lewis) 5:32
Adams, Cleve F., THE BLACK DOOR   (Lewis)   PI:30
Allan, Francis, DEATH IN GENTLE GROVE (Lewis)   PI:29
Anderson, James, THE AFFAIR OF THE BLOOD-STAINED EGG COSY
                                        (Jeff Meyerson) 5:42
Andrews, Mark, BODY RUB   (Arnon Kabatchnik)   5:42
Anthony, Evelyn, THE LEGEND   (Lewis)   1:32
Armstrong, Anthony, THE TRAIL OF FEAR (Charles Shibuk) 4:53
Asimov, Isaac, ASIMOV'S MYSTERIES (Guy M. Townsend)   6:47
———, MURDER AT THE ABA (Martin Morse Wooster)   2:39
Atlee, Philip, THE MAKASSAR STRAIT CONTRACT (Lewis)   3:40
Avallone, Mike, THE CASE OF THE BOUNCING BETTY
                                        (Art Scott)   2:46
———, THE CASE OF THE VIOLENT VIRGIN (Scott)   2:46
Axton, David, PRISON OF ICE   (George Kelley) 6:46
Bagby, George, TWO IN THE BUSH   (Lewis)   PI:25
Bailey, H. C., BLACKLAND, WHITE LAND   (Townsend)   PI:38
———, THE RED CASTLE MYSTERY   (Lewis)   5:35
Ball, John, THE EYES OF BUDDHA   (Lewis)   3:40
———, ditto   (Francis M. Nevins, Jr.) 5:45
———, ed., THE MYSTERY STORY   (Wooster)   2:23
———, ditto   (Scott)   3:32
Ballinger, Bill S., HEIST ME HIGHER   (Meyerson)   4:52
Barns, Glenn M., MURDER IS A GAMBLE   (Lewis)   1:28
Benton, Kenneth, CRAIG AND THE MIDAS TOUCH (Lewis)   PI:29
Berger, Thomas, WHO IS TEDDY VILLANOVA? (Kelley)   4:46
Bergman, Andrew, THE BIG KISS-OFF OF 1944 (Lewis)   3:38
Berkeley, Anthony, TOP STORY MURDER   (Lewis)   1:32
Blanc, Suzanne, THE GREEN STONE (Robert M. Williams)   5:48
Bleeck, Oliver, NO QUESTIONS ASKED   (Nevins)   2:14
Bloch, Robert, THE KING OF TERRORS   (Wooster)   6:43
Block, Lawrence, THE SINS OF THE FATHERS (Meyerson)   2:22
Blom, K. Arne, THE MOMENT OF TRUTH   (Kabatchnik)   4:45
Brett, Simon, CAST, IN ORDER OF DISAPPEARANCE (Lewis) 1:29
———, SO MUCH BLOOD   (Townsend)   5:37
Bronte, Louisa, MOONLIGHT AT GREYSTONE (Lewis)   1:31
Brown, Carter, NEGATIVE IN BLUE   (Stephen Mertz) 4:48
———, THE STRIPPER   (Lewis)   5:34
———, THE WANTON   (Lewis)   PI:26
Brown, Fredric, WE ALL KILLED GRANDMA (Lewis)   2:24
Bruce, Leo, COLD BLOOD   (Shibuk)   1:34
Buchanan, Patrick, A MURDER OF CROWS   (Lewis)   1:28
Burley, W. J., THREE-TOED PUSSY   (Meyerson)   6:52
———, WYCLIFFE AND THE SCHOOLGIRLS (Lewis)   PI:29
Burns, Rex, THE ALVAREZ JOURNAL   (Lewis)   PI:28
———, THE FARNSWORTH SCORE   (Lewis)   5:29
Bush, Christopher, THE CASE OF THE COUNTERFEIT COLONEL
                                        (Lewis)   4:39

Carr, John Dickson, THE CROOKED HINGE (Meyerson)		4:41
———, ditto	(Wooster)	4:41
———, HAG'S NOOK	(Townsend)	PI:35
Carvic, Heron, PICTURE MISS SEETON	(Lewis)	4:38
Charles, Robert, A CLASH OF HAWKS	(Lewis)	PI:23
Charteris, Leslie, THE SAINT IN NEW YORK (Meyerson)		5:46
Chesney, Kellow, THE VICTORIAN UNDERWORLD (Townsend)		PI:34
Cheyney, Peter, DARK INTERLUDE	(Lewis)	PI:27
Childers, Erskine, THE RIDDLE OF THE SANDS (Townsend)		6:49
Clinton-Baddeley, V.C., MY FOE OUTSTRETCHED BENEATH THE TREE		
	(Townsend)	PI:39
Coe, Tucker, WAX APPLES	(Townsend)	PI:21
Cohen, Octavus Roy, THE CORPS THAT WALKED (Shibuk)		6:54
Collins, Max, BAIT MONEY	(Kelley)	6:50
———, BLOOD MONEY	(Kelley)	6:50
———, THE BROKER	(Kelley)	6:50
———, THE BROKER'S WIFE	(Kelley)	6:50
———, THE DEALER	(Kelley)	6:50
Conaway, J. C., THE DEADLY SPRING	(Kabatchnik)	5:41
Coxe, George Harmon, THE GLASS TRIANGLE (Lewis)		5:36
———, WOMAN AT BAY	(Lewis)	2:26
Crane, Frances, THE CINNAMON MURDER	(Lewis)	5:35
Crofts, Freeman Wills, SIR JOHN MAGILL'S LAST JOURNEY		
	(Townsend)	PI:10
Crowe, John, WHEN THEY KILL YOUR WIFE (Lewis)		6:38
Curtis, Mike, THE SAVAGE WOMEN	(Kabatchnik)	5:41
Cushman, Dan, OPIUM FLOWER	(Lewis)	PI:25
Cussler, Clive, RAISE THE TITANIC!	(Kabatchnik)	4:44
Daly, Elizabeth, ARROW POINTING NOWHERE (Townsend)		PI:34
———, DEADLY NIGHTSHADE	(Townsend)	PI:33
Davis, Frederick C., THE DEADLY MISS ASHLEY (Lewis)		1:28
Delving, Michael, THE DEVIL FINDS WORK (Kelley)		6:50
———, DIE LIKE A MAN	(Kelley)	6:50
———, ditto	(Townsend)	PI:37
———, SMILING THE BOY FELL DEAD	(Kelley)	6:50
Deming, Richard, SHE'LL HATE ME TOMORROW (Lewis)		PI:28
Denbie, Roger, DEATH ON THE LIMITED	(Townsend)	PI:38
Dewey, Thomas B., THE TAURUS TRIP	(Lewis)	PI:24
Dietrich, Robert, ANGEL EYES	(Marvin Lachman)	4:51
Douglas, Malcolm, THE DEADLY DAMES	(Lewis)	3:42
———, PURE SWEET HELL	(Lewis)	PI:29
Downing, Warwick, THE GAMBLER, THE MINSTREL, AND THE DANCE		
HALL QUEEN	(Lewis)	1:30
Drummond, Ivor, THE NECKLACE OF SKULLS (Lewis)		6:39
Effinger, George Alec, FELICIA	(Lewis)	2:24
Egan, Lesley, THE BLIND SEARCH	(Myrtis Broset)	4:41
———, ditto	(Lewis)	5:31
Ellin, Stanley, KINDLY DIG YOUR GRAVE	(Nevins)	1:35
Fair, A. A., DOUBLE OR QUITS	(Lewis)	2:23
Fenady, Andrew J., THE MAN WITH BOGART'S FACE (Lewis)		3:39
———, ditto	(Jeff Banks)	3:44
Ferris, Paul, HIGH PLACES	(Lewis)	5:30
Fischer, Bruno, THE FLESH WAS COLD	(Lewis)	1:27
———, QUOTH THE RAVEN	(Lewis)	2:25
Fleming, Joan, . . . TO MAKE AN UNDERWORLD (Lewis)		1:33
Fletcher, Lucille, EIGHTY DOLLARS TO STAMFORD (Lewis)		PI:25
Ford, George, 'GATOR	(Kabatchnik)	3:45

Forrest, Richard, THE WIZARD OF DEATH	(Lewis)	5:29
Foxx, Jack, FREEBOOTY	(Lewis)	2:23
Francis, Dick, KNOCKDOWN	(Lewis)	3:40
Franklin, Max, CHARLIE'S ANGELS	(Lewis)	4:39
Freeborn, Brian, GOOD LUCK MISTER CAIN	(Lewis)	4:37
Freeling, Nicholas, THE BUGLES BLOWING	(Nevins)	5:44
Fuller, Samuel, DEAD PIGEON ON BEETHOVEN STREET	(Lewis)	PI:25
Furst, Alan, YOUR DAY IN THE BARREL	(Lewis)	PI:28
Gardiner, Dorothy & Kathrine Sorley Walker, eds., RAYMOND CHANDLER SPEAKING	(Meyerson)	6:45
Gardner, Erle Stanley, THE CASE OF THE AMOROUS AUNT	(Nevins)	3:49
_____, THE CASE OF THE BEAUTIFUL BEGGAR	(Nevins)	4:54
_____, THE CASE OF THE BIGAMOUS SPOUSE	(Nevins)	1:37
_____, THE CASE OF THE BLONDE BONANZA	(Nevins)	2:10
_____, THE CASE OF THE CARELESS CUPID	(Nevins)	5:50
_____, THE CASE OF THE DARING DIVORCEE	(Nevins)	3:49
_____, THE CASE OF THE FABULOUS FAKE	(Nevins)	5:51
_____, THE CASE OF THE HORRIFIED HEIRS	(Nevins)	3:50
_____, THE CASE OF THE ICE-COLD HANDS	(Nevins)	2:45
_____, THE CASE OF THE MISCHIEVOUS DOLL	(Nevins)	2:45
_____, THE CASE OF THE PHANTOM FORTUNE	(Nevins)	3:50
_____, THE CASE OF THE QUEENLY CONTESTANT	(Nevins)	5:50
_____, THE CASE OF THE RELUCTANT MODEL	(Nevins)	1:37
_____, THE CASE OF THE SHAPELY SHADOW	(Nevins)	1:36
_____, THE CASE OF THE SPURIOUS SPINSTER	(Nevins)	1:36
_____, THE CASE OF THE STEPDAUGHTER'S SECRET	(Nevins)	2:45
_____, THE CASE OF THE TROUBLED TRUSTEE	(Nevins)	4:54
_____, THE CASE OF THE WORRIED WAITRESS	(Nevins)	4:54
Garfield, Brian, RECOIL	(Lewis)	5:34
_____, WHAT OF TERRY CONNISTON?	(Lewis)	2:25
Gifford, Thomas, THE CAVANAUGH QUEST	(Lewis)	3:39
ditto	(Meyerson)	3:04
Gillis, Jackson, THE KILLERS OF STARFISH	(Broset)	6:43
Goulart, Ron, ed., THE HARDBOILED DICKS	(Meyerson)	2:37
Gould, Heywood, ONE DEAD DEBUTANTE	(Lewis)	2:43
Graeme, Bruce, THE DISAPPEARANCE OF ROGER TREMAYNE	(Shibuk)	2:41
Grant, Maxwell, GREEN EYES	(Lewis)	3:42
Gruber, Frank, THE FRENCH KEY MYSTERY	(Meyerson)	5:47
Haggard, William, YESTERDAY'S ENEMY	(Lewis)	4:37
Hall, P. H., IN THE LAMB WHITE DAYS	(Lewis)	PI:30
Hall, Robert Lee, EXIT SHERLOCK HOLMES	(Lewis)	5:51
_____, ditto	(Townsend)	5:51
Hamilton, Donald, THE AMBUSHERS	(Meyerson)	2:38
_____, MURDERERS' ROW	(Meyerson)	5:50
_____, THE RAVAGERS	(Meyerson)	2:38
_____, THE REMOVERS	(Meyerson)	4:53
_____, THE RETALIATORS	(Lewis)	1:30
_____, THE TERRORIZERS	(Townsend)	6:48
Harper, David, THE HANGED MEN	(Lewis)	2:38
Harrison, Chip, MAKE OUT WITH MURDER	(Scott)	2:45
_____, THE TOPLESS TULIP CAPER	(Scott)	2:45
Henderson, Laurence, MAJOR ENQUIRY	(Lewis)	1:47
Heyer, Georgette, THEY FOUND HIM DEAD	(Broset)	6:42
Higgins, Jack, STORM WARNING	(Meyerson)	2:40
Hill, Peter, THE HUNTERS	(Lewis)	3:47

Hilton, John Buxton, GAMEKEEPER'S GALLOWS (Lewis)		6:38
Hitchcock, Alfred, ed., MURDERERS' ROW (Lewis)		1:33
Holding, Elizabeth Sanxay, THE BLANK WALL (Jane S. Bakerman)		5:46
Holman, Hugh, SLAY THE MURDERER	(Lewis)	PI:24
Hunt, E. Howard, WASHINGTON PAYOFF	(Lachman)	4:51
———, WHERE MURDER WAITS	(Lachman)	4:51
Innes, Michael, DEATH BY WATER	(Townsend)	PI:31
———, FROM LONDON FAR	(Broset)	4:48
Jahn, Mike, THE QUARK MANEUVER	(Lewis)	5:31
James, David, CROC	(Kabatchnik)	3:45
James, P. D., SHROUD FOR A NIGHTINGALE (Lewis)		PI:24
Jepson, Edgar, THE GIRL'S HEAD	(Shibuk)	3:43
Kaplan, Arthur, A KILLING FOR CHARITY (Lewis)		PI:27
Katz, Shelley, ALLIGATOR	(Kabatchnik)	3:45
Keene, Day, TAKE A STEP TO MURDER	(Lewis)	PI:26
Kemelman, Harry, WEDNESDAY THE RABBI GOT WET (Meyerson)		4:43
Kenrick, Tony, THE CHICAGO GIRL	(Lewis)	2:24
Knickmeyer, Steve, STRAIGHT	(Lewis)	2:27
———, ditto	(Meyerson)	2:16
Knox, Bill, RALLY TO KILL	(Lewis)	5:36
Kotzwinkle, William, FATA MORGANA	(Kelley)	4:46
Lacy, Ed, SHAKEDOWN FOR MURDER	(Lewis)	PI:27
Landrum, Larry N., Pat Browne & Ray B. Browne, eds.,		
DIMENSIONS OF DETECTIVE FICTION	(Kelley)	4:50
Langton, Jane, THE MINUTEMAN MURDERS	(Broset)	2:41
Lathen, Emma, BY HOOK OR BY CROOK	(Broset)	6:42
Laumer, Keith, FAT CHANCE	(Joe Lansdale)	5:43
Linzee, David, DEATH IN CONNECTICUT	(Lewis)	5:33
Lockridge, Richard, DEAD RUN	(Lewis)	1:28
———, ditto	(Townsend)	PI:36
Lovesey, Peter, A CASE OF SPIRITS	(Townsend)	6:43
———, SWING, SWING TOGETHER	(Lewis)	1:27
Lutz, John, BUYER BEWARE	(Lewis)	4:37
———, ditto	(Nevins)	3:43
Lyons, Arthur, THE DEAD ARE DISCREET	(Lewis)	PI:29
McBain, Ed, DEATH OF A NURSE	(Meyerson)	4:44
———, EVEN THE WICKED	(Broset)	5:40
———, ditto	(Meyerson)	4:44
———, TEN PLUS ONE	(Broset)	4:47
———, WHERE THERE'S SMOKE	(Broset)	5:40
McCloy, Helen, THE CHANGELING CONSPIRACY (Lewis)		6:38
McClure, James, SNAKE	(Kabatchnik)	1:35
Mcdonald, Gregory, CONFESS, FLETCH	(Meyerson)	5:37
———, FLETCH	(Lewis)	3:37
———, ditto	(Meyerson)	5:37
MacDonald, John D., DEAD LOW TIDE	(Lewis)	3:40
———, NIGHTMARE IN PINK	(Meyerson)	3:48
Macdonald, Ross, THE BLUE HAMMER	(Kabatchnik)	2:38
McGraw, Lee, HATCHETT	(Lewis)	2:26
MacKenzie, Donald, DEATH IS A FRIEND	(Lewis)	5:34
Maguire, Michael, SCRATCHPROOF	(Lewis)	6:38
Maling, Arthur, SCHROEDER'S GAME	(Lewis)	5:29
Mara, Bernard, THIS GUN FOR GLORIA	(Lewis)	PI:23
Marcott, James, HARD TO KILL	(Lewis)	PI:26
Martin, Ian Kennedy, THE DEAL OF THE CENTURY (Lewis)		5:33
Masterson, HUNTER OF THE BLOOD	(Lewis)	5:30

Meyers, Martin, SPY AND DIE	(Lewis)	2:24
Millar, Margaret, ASK FOR ME TOMORROW	(Lewis)	4:37
Miller, Victor B. FERNANDA	(Banks)	2:44
Miller, Wade, GUILTY BYSTANDER	(Meyerson)	5:49
Monig, Christopher, ONCE UPON A CRIME	(Lewis)	PI:23
Moore, Robin, THE TERMINAL CONNECTION	(Broset)	5:41
Morrison, Arthur, BEST MARTIN HEWITT DETECTIVE STORIES		
	(Townsend)	5:38
Moyes, Patricia, BLACK WIDOWER	(Townsend)	6:47
Murdoch, Derrick, THE AGATHA CHRISTIE MYSTERY	(Shibuk)	2:4
Murphy, John, PAY ON THE WAY OUT	(Lewis)	1:27
Nielsen, Torben, AN UNSUCCESSFUL MAN	(Lewis)	3:38
O'Donnell, Peter, THE IMPOSSIBLE VIRGIN	(Wooster)	6:54
Olson, Donald, IF I DON'T TELL	(Lewis)	PI:27
Ousby, Ian, BLOODHOUNDS OF HEAVEN	(Nevins)	4:49
Parker, Robert, PASSPORT TO PERIL	(Lewis)	4:40
Parker, Robert B., GOD SAVE THE CHILD	(Townsend)	1:26
_____, PROMISED LAND	(Lewis)	1:32
Patterson, Harry, THE VALHALLA EXCHANGE	(Meyerson)	4:43
Patterson, James, THE THOMAS BERRYMAN NUMBER	(Lewis)	5:33
Peeples, Samuel A., THE MAN WHO DIED TWICE	(Lewis)	3:41
Pentecost, Hugh, DIE AFTER DARK	(Lewis)	2:38
Penzler, Otto, ed., WHODUNIT? HOUDINI?	(Lewis)	PI:31
Perry, Robin, WELCOME FOR A HERO	(Lewis)	1:31
Perry, Will, MURDER AT THE U.N.	(Lewis)	1:33
Philips, Judson, BACKLASH	(Lewis)	PI:31
Pronzini, Bill, BLOWBACK	(Lewis)	5:32
_____, GAMES	(Lewis)	2:25
_____, ed., MIDNIGHT SPECIALS	(Kelley)	6:46
_____, & Barry Malzberg, THE RUNNING OF BEASTS		
	(Kelley)	2:37
_____, ditto	(Nevins)	1:17
Quinn, Seabury, THE ADVENTURES OF JULES DE GRANDIN		
	(Wooster)	2:42
Rabe, Peter, AGREEMENT TO KILL	(Lewis)	2:24
Rendell, Ruth, A DEMON IN MY VIEW	(Lewis)	3:37
Riefe, Alan, TYGER AT BAY	(Lewis)	PI:26
_____, TYGER BY THE TAIL	(Lewis)	PI:29
Rinehart, Mary Roberts, THE CIRCULAR STAIRCASE	(Wooster)	5:38
Robeson, Kenneth, THE EVIL GNOME	(Lewis)	PI:24
Roper, L. V., HOOKERS DON'T GO TO HEAVEN	(Lewis)	2.26
Ross, Hal, THE FLEUR-DE-LIS AFFAIR	(Lewis)	1:30
Ross, Jonathan, THE BURNING OF BILLY TOOBER	(Lewis)	PI:28
Rossiter, John, THE MURDER MAKERS	(Lewis)	6:39
_____, THE VILLAINS	(Lewis)	1:28
Rovin, Jeff, HOLLYWOOD DETECTIVE: GARRISON	(Lachman)	1:34
Royce, Kenneth, BUSTILLO	(Lewis)	3:38
Ruhm, Herbert, ed., THE HARD-BOILED DETECTIVE	(Lachman)	2:34
_____, ditto	(Lewis)	2:35
Russell, A. J., POUR THE HEMLOCK	(Lewis)	3:37
Ryck, Francis, SACRIFICIAL PAWN	(Townsend)	PI:34
_____, THE SERN CHARTER	(Lewis)	PI:30
Sadler, Mark, CIRCLE OF FIRE	(Broset)	4:47
_____, ditto	(Meyerson)	3:37
St. John, David, RETURN FROM VORKUTA	(Lachman)	4:31
Sapir, Richard & Warren Murphy, HOLY TERROR	(Meyerson)	3:9
_____, IN ENEMY HANDS	(Lewis)	2:3

_____, LAST WAR DANCE	(Meyerson)	3:48
_____, MAFIA FIX	(Meyerson)	6:52
Saxon, Alex, RUN IN DIAMONDS	(Lewis)	6:40
Scherf, Margaret, IF YOU WANT A MURDER WELL DONE	(Lewis)	PI:26
Seaman, Donald, THE TERROR SYNDICATE	(Lewis)	4:38
Sheldon, Sidney, THE NAKED FACE	(Meyerson)	3:47
Shirreffs, Gordon R., THE MARAUDERS	(Lewis)	3:41
Simenon, Georges, MAIGRET AND THE BLACK SHEEP	(Nevins)	5:44
Simmel, Johannes Mario, THE CAESAR CODE	(Lewis)	1:29
Mimmons, Geoffrey I., THE Z PAPERS	(Broset)	6:42
Singer, Norman, DIAMOND STUD	(Lewis)	2:28
_____, THE SHAKEDOWN KID	(Lewis)	2:27
Smith, Elizabeth Foote, GENTLE ALBATROSS	(Broset)	2:42
Smith, Myron J., Jr., CLOAK-AND-DAGGER BIBLIOGRAPHY	(Nevins)	4:50
Spain, Nancy, DEATH GOES ON SKIS	(Lewis)	6:40
Spewack, Samuel, MURDER IN THE GILDED CAGE	(Shibuk)	5:48
Spillane, Mickey, MY GUN IS QUICK	(Lewis)	PI:28
Stark, Richard, THE SOUR LEMON SCORE	(Meyerson)	6:51
Stein, Aaron Marc, COFFIN COUNTRY	(Lewis)	6:39
_____, DAYS OF MISFORTUNE	(Bakerman)	6:52
Steinbrunner, Chris & Otto Penzler, eds., ENCYCLOPEDIA OF MYSTERY & DETECTION	(Scott)	PI:13
Stout, Rex, PLOT IT YOURSELF	(Lewis)	PI:23
Symons, Julian, A THREE-PIPE PROBLEM	(Meyerson)	3:48
Talbot, Hake, RIM OF THE PIT	(Meyerson)	5:49
Thornburg, Newton, CUTTER AND BONE	(Meyerson)	4:43
Tracy, Don, HIGH, WIDE AND RANSOM	(Lewis)	2:28
Upfield, Arthur W., AN AUTHOR BITES THE DUST	(Townsend)	PI:32
_____, JOURNEY TO THE HANGMAN	(Townsend)	PI:32
_____, THE NEW SHOE	(Scott)	2:33
_____, ditto	(Wooster)	2:32
Van de Wetering, Janwillem, THE CORPSE ON THE DIKE	(Lewis)	1:30
_____, TUMBLEWEED	(Broset)	2:42
Vidal, Gore, MATTERS OF FACT AND FICTION: ESSAYS 1973-1976	(Kelley)	5:39
Washburn, Mark, THE ARMAGEDDON GAME	(Lewis)	5:33
Weill, Gus, A WOMAN'S EYES	(Keith Ekblaw)	1:11
Weston, Carolyn, ROUSE THE DEVIL	(Lewis)	1:29
Winslow, Pauline Glen, THE BRANDENBURG HOTEL	(Broset)	2:42
_____, ditto	(Lewis)	1:31
Winsor, Roy, THREE MOTIVES FOR MURDER	(Lewis)	2:26
Wolfe, Michael, THE CHINESE FIRE DRILL	(Nevins)	2:40
Woods, Sara, THE LAW'S DELAY	(Broset)	4:48
_____, ditto	(Lewis)	5:29
_____, MY LIFE IS DONE	(Lewis)	4:38
Wright, Laurie Robeson, THE PERFECT CORPSE	(Broset)	4:47
Yarbro, Chelsea Quinn, OGILVIE, TALLANT & MOON	(Lewis)	4:39
York, Andrew, THE FASCINATOR	(Lewis)	5:35
_____, THE INFILTRATOR	(Townsend)	PI:16

THE NERO WOLFE SAGA

Part V

By Guy M. Townsend

"Home to Roost" [July-August 1951], published in *Triple Jeopardy*, 1952.
    THE STORY ::: Wolfe is hired by Mr. and Mrs. Benjamin Rackell (Rackell Importing Company) to investigate the murder of their nephew, Arthur Rackell, by means of the insertion of a potassium cyanide capsule into his vitamin box. Arthur had been a loud-mouthed communist and he eventually became so obnoxious that his aunt ordered him out of her home. Arthur then confided to her that he was really working as an undercover agent for the FBI, whereupon Mrs. Rackell relented and let him stay. When he was murdered shortly thereafter, Mrs. Rackell was dissatisfied with the job being done by the police and the FBI, who she informed of her displeasure, and so she came to Wolfe. A passable, but not outstanding entry.
    WOLFE ::: Wolfe's disliking for work continues unabated: "He would have loved to tell her to get lost. But his house had five stories, counting the basement and the plant rooms full of orchids on the roof, and there was Fritz the chef and Theodore the botanist and me, Archie Goodwin, the fairly confidential assistant, with nothing to carry the load but his income as a private detective." In this episode Wolfe has a beer after his morning session, which may be the first mention of a pre-lunch beer. After a harrowing experience in the office regarding a woman (see below) Wolfe flees into the kitchen where Archie later finds him standing, "a slice of sturgeon in one hand and a glass of beer in the other" (he later eats a melon as well), which leads Archie to ask, "what about your rule on not eating at bed-time?" On the subject of eating, we are informed that Wolfe detests oysters with horseradish on them. Wolfe's weight, incidentally, is said to be one-seventh of a ton in this episode. The above-mentioned harrowing experience cannot but have strengthened Wolfe's aversion to women: a woman deliberately sweeps a bowl of orchids off Wolfe's desk onto the floor, then "she brought the bottle of Scotch along and poured a good three fingers in Wolfe's beer glass. She put the bottle on his desk, leaned over to stretch an arm and pat him on top of the head, straightened up, and grinned at him." Wolfe "glared at her", and then fled from the room. It's enough to make any man a misogynist. The story gives Wolfe an opportunity to make several remarks about communists: "It is true that all five of these people may be communists and therefore enemies of this country, but that does not justify framing one of them for murder"; "You know the opinion of communism held by most Americans, including me"; "I deplore the current tendency to accuse people of pro-communism irresponsibly and unjustly." Lastly, Wolfe works the London *Times* crossword puzzle again, and he continues to use the word "jackassery".
    ARCHIE ::: Wolfe asks Archie how a male suspect feels about a female suspect--"It's a serious question in a field where you are qualified as an expert and I'm not." Archie's commendable efforts to maintain his expert's qualifications are evident in the following: "Whenever we have a flock of guests I handle the seating, and if there is one who seems worthy of study I put her in the chair nearest mine". Speaking of "the headquarters of the Homicide Squad, Manhattan West", Archie says, "They have never let me roam loose in that building since the day I took a snapshot of a piece of paper they were saving, though they couldn't

prove it." Archie uses another ethnic slur in this one (the first in quite a while), though it's used in fun--he tells Fred Durkin that he's "my favorite mick." Archie's notebook is again in use, and he gives his weight as 180 pounds. And here's something about Archie that pleases me greatly: "Nothing would have been more appreciated right then than a large coke-and-lime with the ice brushing my lips."

OTHER REGULARS ::: "Saul Panzer, the one guy I want within hearing the day I get hung on the face of a cliff with jet eagles zooming at me. With his saggy shoulders and his face all nose, he looks one-fifth as strong and hardy, and one-tenth as smart, as he really is." Wolfe says, "Mr. Panzer's quality is known." The good inspector shows up: "Cramer had been holding in with difficulty. Holding in is a chronic problem with him, and it shows in various ways, chiefly by his big red face getting redder, with the color spreading lower on his thick muscular neck." "Sergeant Purley Stebbins was big and strong but not handsome." Neither Cramer nor Stebbins play much of a role in this one, nor do Lon Cohen or Lt. Rowcliff, who are just mentioned. Fred and Orrie (together with Saul) are hauled in to do foot work. Herb Aronson and his cab show up again, and Fritz is present, mostly on the periphery, as usual.

PHYSICAL ASPECTS ::: The one-way glass panel in the front door is mentioned again (why do I persist in noticing this?), also "the red leather chair at the end of Wolfe's desk", and "the table by the big globe, which Fritz and I had outfitted [with drinks for the guests]."

ROUTINE AT THE BROWNSTONE ::: "There has never been a dog in that house."

ODDS AND ENDS ::: The FBI has a small role in this one (because of the communist angle). The agent involved is named Wengert, with whom Archie had served in G-2 during the war. He is completely unhelpful, though he admits "I'll never forget how he [Wolfe] came through on that mercury thing." "That mercury thing", by the way, is not a part of the recorded Saga.

"The Cop-Killer" [Summer 1951], published in *Triple Jeopardy*, 1952.
THE STORY ::: What looks at first like a fairly simple matter of protecting two illegal immigrants from the folly of their over-developed apprehension of policemen turns serious when the cop in question turns up dead with a pair of scissors stuck in his back and the two foreigners tucked away in the brownstone's front room, are the prime suspects. Carl and Tina Vardas fled from the Goldenrod Barber Shop where they were both employed immediately after being questioned, along with all of the shop's other employees, by a plain-clothes cop. When Archie drops by the shop to get a line on what's going on he finds the cops in possession and investigating the murder of one of their own. This puts the boys in the brownstone in an unenviable position, but all problems are solved when Wolfe exposes the murderer through an outstanding bit of fair play deduction. One of the better short stories in the Saga.

WOLFE ::: This is slightly out of place here, but it doesn't fit conveniently anywhere else either, so we might as well tackle it here and now and get done with it. When Wolfe's regular barber, a man named Fletcher, retired two years earlier, he tried the Goldenrod Barber Shop, which Archie had at that time patronized for four years. He did not like the way Archie's barber, Ed Graboff, worked, and he finally settled down with Jimmy Kirk, and "his position now, after two years, was that Jimmy was no Fletcher, especially with a shampoo, but that he was better than tolerable." The shop, which is run by Joel Fickler, is located "in the basement of an office building on Lexington Avenue in the upper Thirties," and Wolfe actually walks to it in this episode, and may in fact do so whenever he needs barbering, given his aversion to wheeled vehicles. Wolfe, incidentally, has his hair cut with scissors-- "Wolfe barred clippers." A couple of Wolfe's familiar eccentricities and peculiarities are present in this outing: "Wolfe would rather be in a room with a hungry tiger than with a woman out of hand [i.e. crying, or hysterical];" "And then his lips in their familiar movement, pushed out and then pulled in, out and in again, which meant he had accepted the inevitable and was getting the machinery going. I had seen him like that for an hour at a stretch." But here is a new item: "He leaned back, closed his eyes, and heaved a deep sigh, and from the way his nose began to twitch I knew he was coercing himself into facing the hard fact that he would have to go to work." Archie also tells us that "he had a strong prejudice against entertaining murderers at his table. Some years back a female prospective client had dined with us in an emergency, on roast Waterhouse goose. It turned out that she was a husband-poisoner, and roast goose had been off our menue for a solid year, though Wolfe was very fond of it." Wolfe himself remarks, "I call few men, and no women, by their first names." He also gives us his views on mountain climbing: "I cannot agree that mountain climbing is merely one manifestation of man's spiritual aspirations. I think instead it is an hysterical paroxym of his infantile vanity." Of Wolfe's intelligence Archie says, "I have never tried to deny that the interior decorator did a snappier job inside his skull than in mine." Archie also mentions Wolfe's one-seventh of a ton, but says "Wolfe can move when he wants to. I have seen him prove it more than once." It seems to be a well-established Wolfe custom to ring for beer immediately upon coming down from the morning session in the plant rooms, and Archie elsewhere speaks of Wolfe's "fixed allotment, three bottles of beer" after lunch. Lastly, Wolfe's nationality is in question again, as he himself remarks, "I got my naturalization papers twenty-four years ago." Though supporting his statement in *Too Many Cooks* that he was not born in this country, this contradicts his later statement that he is a native American and, elsewhere, that he has voted for three decades. Ah, Nero Wolfe, why all this obfuscation? Wolfe says "pfui" in this one.

ARCHIE ::: At last a birthplace for Archie: Chillicothe, Ohio. But that, and his assertion that he is constantly badgering Wolfe for a raise, is about all for Archie this time out.

OTHER REGULARS ::: Archie gives us another description of Cramer-- "broad shouldered husky, gray-haired and gray-eyed, with an unlit cigar slanting up from a corner of his mouth"--and say s, "I have to admit he's a good cop." Archie also calls him "the man to fix the chair." Wolfe and Cramer never really start going at each other in this one. At one point Cramer says he doesn't believe something that Wolfe has told him, and wolfe says, "Then you don't. I'm not responsible for your credulity quotient." As usual, Cramer initially turns down Wolfe's offer of beer, but later he changes his mind: "I guess I'll have a little beer after all, if you don't mind. I'm tired." And Archie says, "Unlike Wolfe, he didn't care for a lot of foam." Finally, Wolfe and Archie take advantage of Cramer's habitual distrust of everything they tell him to bluff him into believing that the clients were not in the front room when in fact they were. "My old friend and enemy Sergeant Purley Stebbins" is more visible than usual in this one, and he is described by a woman in the case as "that big one with the big ears and gold tooth." He calls Archie by his first name in this episode, which leads Archie to remark, "The nature of my encounters with him usually had him calling me Goodwin, but occasionally it was Archie." Fritz only appears once, to bring Wolfe his beer, and there are no other familiar faces, unless you count General Carpenter in Washington, who is just mentioned on the last page.

PHYSICAL ASPECTS ::: Not much this time: the seven steps of the front stoop are again mentioned; "the first door to the left of the long wide hall was to what we ca-led the front room"; the front room is still soundproofed and "the windows have bars."

ODDS AND ENDS ::: At the beginning of this episode Archie speaks of "a complicated infringement case [which] had been polished off for a big client." Archie spends 75¢ for a haircut.

"The Squirt and the Monkey" [Winter 1951-1952], published in *Triple Jeopardy*, 1952.

THE STORY ::: Harry Koven, whose Dazzle Dan comic strip is syndicated throughout the country, offers Wolfe $500 for the loan of Archie and his gun for a few hours. Koven is missing a Marley .32 which he normally kept in a drawer in his desk, and he wants Archie's help (and that of Archie's Marley) in bluffing out which ever of the other five members of his household has taken it. Things do not, however, go exactly according to plan, and one member of the household ends up murdered with Archie's gun. As usual, Cramer behaves like a perfect ass towards Archie and Wolfe, before the latter saves his bacon for him. The ending is rather peculiar and, uncharacteristically, not very satisfactory. This is not one of Stout's better efforts in the short form, though there is a neat little clue hidden in a comic strip.

WOLFE ::: Wolfe is in the 85% income tax bracket, and he gives $100,000 as a modest estimate of his average annual income. He works the London *Times* crossword puzzle in this one and says "pfui", "morass and fatuity", and "conjugal privities". He also speaks of "the jackassery of Mr. Cramer." Wolfe's lip routine is mentioned as evidence of cerebral activity, which is familiar. But here is something new: "He was in a nasty humor. He hated to work right after dinner, and from the way he kept his chin down and a slight twitch of a muscle in his cheek I knew it was going to be real work." His antipathy for women is mentioned a couple of times: "He seldom welcomes a man crossing his threshold; he never welcomes a woman"; "Once in a while Wolfe rises when a woman enters his office." He breaks with routine twice in this episode. When Cramer arrives while "guests" are in the brownstone Wolfe actually dons topcoat and hat and steps outside the front door and down the stoop in definitely inclement winter weather to talk to him. And he breaks his morning routine--"breakfast in his room, with the morning papers, at eight; then shaving and dressing; then from nine to eleven, his morning shift up in the pland rooms. He never went to the office before eleven, and the detective business was never allowed to mingle with orchids"--by sneaking down to the office to get some material to work on while Archie is having breakfast in the kitchen.

ARCHIE ::: Archie gets to spend the night in jail in this one. One of his weapons, which he keeps in a drawer in his desk, is a Marley .32, for which he has an armpit holster. His "man about the chair" alias for Cramer is used again.

OTHER REGULARS ::: Cramer is present at his most unpleasant; he even tells Wolfe he is going to lift his license (and means it). Purley is around, too, and Archie gives us another description of him. "He lifted his head and regarded me, perfectly friendly. A perfectly friendly look from Stebbins would, for almost anyone else, cause you to get your guard up and be ready to either duck or counter, but Purley wasn't responsible for the design of his big bony face and his pig-bristle eyebrows." And so is "Lieutenant Rowcliff, whose murder I will not have to premeditate when I get around to it because I have already done the premeditating." Naturally, Archie does his stuttering routine with him. Fritz is around, and Doc Vollmer and Theodore are mentioned. Lon Cohen makes an appearance and we learn that he has 19 years until he retires, so he's probably in his mid-forties. Wolfe makes use of Saul who, he says, "can get in anywhere and do anything." And Wolfe's lawyer Parker, "the only lawyer Wolfe would admit to the bar if he had the say", is utilized several times. The odd thing is that his name is now *Henry George* Parker, not Nathaniel! He has a "long pale face" and he laughs "Haw haw."

PHYSICAL ASPECTS ::: The seven steps of the stoop are again mentioned, as are the one-way panel and the peephole (said to be "in a nook at the end of the hall" covered by a sliding panel on the hall side of the wall). The "button at the edge of [Wolfe's] desk" is mentioned (as being used to summon Fritz), and this item makes its first appearance: a "large mirror on the far wall of the office."

ROUTINE AT THE BROWNSTONE ::: "The doorbell rang. When visitors were present Fritz usually answered the door", from which one may infer that at other times Archie handled it. Archie "used my key but found that the chain bolt was on, which was normal but not invariable when I was out of the house." Finally, "My daytime formula [for answering the phone] was, 'Nero Wolfe's office, Archie Goodwin speaking'." His nighttime formula is not given.

FOR SALE: Crime/Mystery Fiction. All wants searched free of charge. Try me!   S. B. Johns
                                12 Forest View
                                Neath, S. Wales
                                Great Britain

DETECTIVE FICTION LIST available--Michael Cropper Books, 19 Shellwood Road, London, S. W. 11, England.

FREE LIST of paperback mysteries of the 1940's and 1950's available upon request. Want lists welcomed. Will trade for hero pulps and back issues of THE ARMCHAIR DETECTIVE. Steve Smallman, 16600 S.E. 17th St., Bellevue, WA 98008. Sample Dell mapback only $1.50.

THE LINE-UP

The Adventuresses of Sherlock Holmes (Newsletter of B.S.I scion society, edited by Kate Karlson; subscriptions, $2.00 for four issues, from Mary Ellen Cochon, 52 West 56th Street, New York, NY 10019).

The Armchair Detective (An absolute must for any serious mystery fan; edited by Al Hubin, this quarterly is $10.00 per year; subscription address, TAD, 243 12th St., Drawer P, Del Mar, CA 92014).

The Baker Street Journal (Quarterly, $10.00 per year; Fordham University Press, Bronx, NY 10458).

Baker Street Miscellanea (Quarterly, $4.00 per year; The Sciolist Press, P. O. Box 2579, Chicago, IL 60690).

Current Crime (Quarterly, 50p. each; 20 pages of reviews of mysteries published in Britain; Box 18, Bognor Regis, Sussex, PO22 7AA, UK).

Dast Magazine (Unfortunately, this excellent magazine is written almost entirely in Swedish; every once in a while an English language article slips through, but unless you read Swedish this won't be of much use to you; for subscription information write editor Iwan Hedman-Morelius, Flodins väg 5, S-152 00 Strängnäs, Sweden).

The Mystery Monitor (News/Info/Advertising Supplement to *The Mystery Nook*; very irregular, though supposedly monthly; for subscription information write Don Miller, 12315 Judson Rd., Wheaton, MD 20906).

The Mystery Nook (Allegedly quarterly, also from Don Miller).

The Poisoned Pen (Jeff Meyerson, of 50 1st Place, Brooklyn, NY 11231, is turning his DAPA-EM apazine into a general circulation fanzine, the first issue of which should be ready soon; $5.00 for six issues.)

The Pontine Dossier (Annual, edited and published by Luther Norris, 3844 Watseka Avenue, Culver City, CA 90230).

The Rohmer Review (Published irregularly, usually two issues per year; subscriptions, $2.25 for a series of 3 issues by 3rd class mail, or $2.75 for 3 issues via 1st class mail, or $3.00 for 3 issues overseas; edited and published by Robert E. Briney, 4 Forest Avenue, Salem, MA 01970).

The Thorndyke File (2 issues per year, $5.00; from Philip T. Asdell, R.R. #5, Box 355, Frederick, MD 21701).

Xenophile ("A Monthly Advertiser & Journal Devoted to Fantastic and Imaginative Literature"; U.S. subscriptions $12.00 & $6.00 for 1st class and bulk rate respectively, from Nils Hardin, Box 9660, St. Louis, MO 63122).

DAPA-EM: See "MYSTERIOUSLY SPEAKING . . ." in this issue.

MYSTERY*FILE

Short Reviews by Steve Lewis

Stephen Barlay, *Blockbuster* (Morrow; c. 1976; 1st published in U.S., 1977; 336 pp.).
    The first half of this unusually constructed adventure thriller centers about a million-pound threat to blow up a sunken ship near the mouth of the Thames, a leftover from World War II containing thousands of tons of unsalvageable bombs and TNT. Only after the money's been paid, 200 pages later, can the real detective work begin, and the more that's uncovered, the greater and deeper the scope of the scheme is seen to be. The clutter of maps and diagrams and technical jargon adds a necessary amount of verisimilitude to the story as it first appears, but the main theme is actually one of police corruption and the crumbling morale of Scotland Yard. Part two is gripping and violent, and the intricate plotting is more than double the worth of the commercialized suspense that precedes it. (B)*

David Williams, *Unholy Writ* (St. Martin's; c. 1976; 192 pp.).
    An old mansion in Oxfordshire, recently sold to the founder of the Forward Britain Movement, an organization somewhat to the right of Ghenghis Khan, may or may not hold in hiding a lost Shakespearean manuscript, but the possibility is a sure source of high-spirited intrigue. A local vicar who takes his vows of servitude literally and a flock of jibbering Filipinos laboring over what purports to be a swimming pool are only two facets of a delicious tongue-in-tooth British humor—it's not quite tongue-in-cheek, but the merest slip of the tongue would do it. Midst all the swirl of confusion there are few real surprises in store, but it's all undeniably charming, with a happily-ever-after ending to be cherished. (B minus)*

Edward D. Hoch, ed., *Best Detective Stories of the Year—1977* (31st Annual Collection, E. P. Dutton; c. 1977; 198 + x pp.).
    It's undoubtedly been said before about one of the books in this long-running series, but a better title for the one at hand would be something like *Some Pretty Good Mystery Stories from 1976*. There's not much detection in most of these offerings, and only a couple of them did I find particularly outstanding. Avram Davidson's "Crazy Old Lady" comes up with a nifty scheme for combatting urban gorillas in today's crime-ridden streets; and in "November Story" Barbara Callahan tells how a politician's wife nearly escapes her life in limbo—but only by the longest stretch of the term could it even be called a crime story.
    Overall, a well-varied selection representative of all kinds of mystery stories. Something for everyone, plus an excellent summary of the year's events in crime fiction. (B)

---

* Reviews so marked have appeared earlier in the *Hartford Courant*.

Leonard Holton, *A Corner of Paradise* (St. Martin's; c. 1977; 149 pp.).

Father Bredder worries when Lt. Minardi's daughter defiantly marries a black with a criminal record, and all his fears seem justified when the young would-be playright's jacket is found at the scene of a bungled jewel robbery that ends in murder.

A quietly religious mystery novel, not in the sense of any particular organized religion, but concerned with the kind of faith that even with doubts can comfort in many ways. Father Bredder bases his deductions on what he calls spiritual fingerprints, but they also depend to greatly on inspired guesswork and, as quite unfairly revealed later, the *Encyclopedia Brittanica*. Considering it as a mystery story only, I'd have to say I found it disappointing. (C minus)*

David Delman, *The Nice Murderers* (Morrow; c. 1977; 240 pp.).

William and Lizzie Winters are mere dabblers in crime, nicer than Bonnie and Clyde, a charming couple really, but when surprised while cleaning out a safe full of jewels, they discover that they're also capable of murder. The victim is a man aptly nicknamed Piggy, however, and not nearly so well liked.

Very much not the usual sort of crime story and very nearly unmatched in slow sexy urbanity. Unfortunately, Dalman seems to have been terribly confused over what day a second killing is scheduled for, and a good deal of skillful plotting comes close to being completely undone. (B minus)*

Pauline Glen Winslow, *The Witch Hill Murders* (St. Martin's; c. 1977; 250 pp.).

I find the antics of cult-followers awfully tedious, and dislike finding them cluttering the pages of my mystery fiction. The Sidereans' religious fervor spreads through England like the plague, and when they establish a center for learning in the small village of Daines Barington, conflict between town and "gown" quite predictably results in murder.

To his credit, Superintendent Capricorn does a capable job of investigation, but he is, after all, the son of a vaudeville magician, and the obvious opportunity for misdirection should be taken in his stride. Winslow tends toward overwriting, however, and does only half a job in hiding a murderer's identity. (C plus)*

J. F. Burke, *The Kama Sutra Tango* (Harper & Row; c. 1977; 184 pp.).

A partner in a New York City nightclub is murdered, and plenty of dirt comes to light. His previously unsuspected hobby was taking private pornographic movies, the object being blackmail, of course, so there's no scarcity of likely suspects. Doing all of the detective work is the other partner, a piano player set up for a frame and forced to do his deducting on the run.

I'd call it phony tough. Times Square is appropriately sleazy, but the characters are all worn-out stereotypes, and the surrounding atmosphere strikes me as rather cursory, with no particular attempt being made to rise above the obvious. The bloody ending contains no surprises and will surely offend any detective buff still in the audience. (D)

Mel Arrighi, *Turkish White* (Harcourt Brace Jovanovich; c. 1977; 182 pp.).

On the face of it, this is just another everyday drug-smuggling caper, with the good guys one jump behind the bad guys all the way from Turkey to Marseilles. But on the job is a Justice Department official who's trying to live down the John Mitchell days in the face of the anti-US *la dolce vita* attitudes prevailing in Rome and strangely enough finding the same idealism only in Mike Jarrett, the ex-radical now carrying raw opium across Europe, his first run. Active in veterans' groups protesting the war, Jarrett lost his college teaching position because of some anonymous letters sent by the FBI. It's no surprise he's now bitter and cynical.

Democracy, composed of decent-minded individuals, can be made to work, but without proper coordination, it can also leave sour dreams and permanent scars behind.. Arrighi points this out and fingers some of the culprits, but he still manages to keep the proper perspective on the story that quietly makes this one of the suspense novels of the year. If you've ever suffered from the post-Vietnam Watergate blues, this book just might sneak up on you. (A plus)

Elizabeth Lemarchand, *Step in the Dark* (Walker & Co.; c. 1976; 1st published in U.S.A., 1977; 173 pp.).

Death by misadventure occurs in the august halls of the Ramsden Literary and Scientific Society, as a librarian's assistant takes a fatal plunge from the top of a treacherous spiral staircase. However, the accident occurred after hours, a set of valuable books is missing, and a little investigation by Superintendent Pollard shows that now and then the dead woman stooped to petty blackmail.

Puzzle stories are an uncommon species these days, but the British seem to do them well. This one's amply clued and will please any armchair detective, but occasionally things are what we're told, not what we're shown. (C plus)

Collin Wilcox, *Doctor, Lawyer* . . . (Random House; c. 1976; 177 pp.).

San Francisco continually seems to attract all sorts of unusual police cases, in fiction as well as those of the newspaper headline variety. Lieutenant Hastings works for Homicide, and his latest headache is a series of alphabetical nursery rhyme killings. Extortion money is demanded of the city, but the sequence of murders seems to be headed straight for Chief Dwyer.

Pulled into the investigation are the various radical revolutionaries, drug pushers and gunrunners that find a natural habitat in the Bay Area and its unhealthy sections of bottomless massage porno parlors, but unexpectedly the twisted trail heads itself in the opposite direction instead Hastings leans more to single-handed television heroics than one expects from standard police procedurals, and too many characters are neurotics in desperate need of analysis, but the chase itself generates plenty of sarchair excitement. (B minus)

Michael Delving, *The China Expert* (Scribners; c. 1976; 208 pp.).
Delving's previous books have been about an American antique dealer who happens to keep stumbling across murder mysteries while tracking down valuable manuscripts and *objets d'art* in England, in this way providing for us a good deal of enjoyment in viewing British life through American eyes. This time, however, an American agent in Chinese porcelain is drawn into the mysterious world of spies and agents and counteragents when a priceless Chinese vase is stolen from a London museum. What's at stake is the future of British-Chinese relations.
Suddenly all of his friends have their little secrets, their little deceptions. It's a kind of puzzle plotting that's nicely sized down to personal level, but it's also one which does require a lucky amateur indeed to make the pieces fit safely. Sadly, too, while weaving his framework of intrigue, Delving uses up the room that might have better utilized the London background. It could have been New York. (B minus)

Elizabeth Foote-Smith, *Never Say Die* (G. P. Putnam's; c. 1977; 224 pp.).
This book has to be the only one of its kind. Will Woodfield is a private detective. Nothing strange there. His apprentice-assistant is a 21-year-old swinger named Mercy Newcastle, with whom he carries on, in near icky-poo fashion, a "will she? does she?" romance. But that's probably been done before. What *is* unusual is the method of homicide--apparently psychiatrist Graham Baird has been killed by preventing him from returning to his body while on an OOBE--a psychic "out of body experience." Astral travel?
It has a fluffy kind of humor that may grow on you. Not much in the way of surprises, as detective stories go, but yes, definitely mind-expanding. (C plus)

Helen McCloy, *The Imposter* (Dodd, Mead; c. 1977; 180 pp.).
Marina Skinner's automobile accident was not fatal, but she awakes into a world of nightmarish unreality, her world upsidedown, a prisoner unable to leave the hospital. Her version of the accident is denied, there was no other driver, she must have been drinking, she never was pregnant. Her only means of escape is with the man who says that he is her husband--but who indeed is not.
Without any doubt this will tickle any paranoid fancies that you may think hidden safely away, but unfortunately two-thirds of a book, no matter how gripping, just won't do. Quite possibly no ending could adequately explain how Marina's life could be turned so inside out overnight, but this mismash of spies and science fiction will convince mighty few. (C)

Angus Ross, *The Ampurias Exchange* (Walker; c. 1977; 1st published in U.S., 1977; 184 pp.).

Basque terrorists in Spain grab a British intelligence agent and demand as ransom the release of their leader, now in a Scottish prison. Whitehall is naturally reluctant to do so, and instead sends in Mark Farrow to salvage any losses. All it comes down to is some pretty ordinary spy stuff, with plenty of gratuitous violence and hints of major surprises that never come off. (C minus)*

Stuart Kaminsky, *Bullet for a Star* (St. Martin's; c. 1977; 188 pp.).

The year 1940 was a good one for movie fans, and as we tag along with private eye Toby Peters as he hunts for a blackmailer and a killer at the Warner Brothers studios, we're treated to an insider's view of the Golden Age of stars. The case begins with a photograph, no surprise here, this one a scorcher of Errol Flynn and a very, very young girl, and it ends with a final burst of derring-do on the set of the about-to-be-made remake of a picture called "The Maltese Falcon."

It is a great deal of fun, to be sure, and undoubtedly Kaminski had even more, dropping at every opportunity the names of the famous and the not-yet famous, but it is not altogether convincing. One suspects that even sincere love affairs with Hollywood can be all to easily exploited. (B-)

Frank Branston, *An Up and Coming Man* (St. Martins; c. 1977; First published in U.S., 1977; 195 pp.).

If a mystery novel doesn't have a hard-bitten private eye to poke his nose into dirty corners that need it, a tough pertinacious reporter with an ear for scandal will do just as nicely. What Tommy Tompkins, chief reporter for the *Ripley Guardian*, uncovers about the city council's shady dealings in real estate quickly and unexpectedly costs him his job, sets him up in court as a fall guy, and not so incidentally causes the death of three people.

The British evidently have a much more cynical view of local government than do we in this country. Corruption runs deep in Ripley, and there's plenty of satisfaction realized from purposely turning over rocks just to see what scurries for cover. (B)

Jon A. Jackson, *The Diehard* (Random House; c. 1977; 215 pp.).

Detroit's a notoriously violent city, having one of the highest murder rates in the country, and I have to wonder why it's not the scene of more mystery novels than it is. While Sergeant Mulheisen is nominally a precinct detective, he finds plenty to do working for Homicide as well.

The current victim is the wife of a corporation lawyer being investigated in a mammoth insurance fraud. Besides a missing twenty million dollars to attract the interest of the Mob, the manhunt is severely hampered by a Christmas blizzard that completely shuts down the city. The final shootout occurs not far from my hometown in the north-central part of the state, which is probably as close as Cadillac will come to being in a book, but I get a kick out of familiar landmarks.

This is Jackson's first novel, and it's a good one. Mulheisen is pushing forty, unmarried and works on the theory that understanding human relationships is the key to solving most crimes. Along the way we get a good look at his own vague feelings of self-doubt, which provide the kind of interest in the detective as a person that will make a reader come back for more. (A minus)*

Lionel Derrick, *Devine Death* (Pinnacle 40-085; c. 1977; 149 pp.).

All that this imitation Executioner series really has going for it is momentum. A lot of similar series have come and gone in recent years, but somehow this is already the 23rd adventure of Mark Hardin, alias "The Penetrator". Considering the total sales figures compiled by this and such other series as "The Butcher", "The Death Merchant", and the like, there must be a whole other fandom out there!

To be honest, this one is different from the usual bang-bang-shoot-the-Mafia type of story. Here Hardin's target is the newly formed Church of the Final Coming, which is doing a bang-up job of converting the youth of America, thanks in part to one of those liberalistic, bureaucratic rulings that drive right-wing fanatics right up the wall. There are even hints--well, more than hints--that funny business is going on with the young female initiates. What Hardin doesn't expect to learn while cleansing the temple is that the secret masterminds behind the phoney church are really planning to take over the country by assassinating nearly anyone of importance.

No, I'm not telling you anything I shouldn't, assuming that you'd read the back cover before the book anyway. If you haven't spotted it yet, the plot comes straight from the glory days of pulp fiction, updated of course with all the cliches of television. A couple of interesting story lines do develop, but they die quickly for lack of nourishment. What's left is non-stop action that requires no active participation on the part of the reader--that's what's promised, and that's what's delivered. Presumably the reader knows what side he's to cheer for. (D)

Janice Law, *Gemini Trip* (Houghton Mifflin; c. 1977; 179 pp.).

Anna Peters' task, as a member of New World Oil's research department, is to find the missing feminine half of a pair of young tempermental twins about to inherit a sizable chunk of New World stock. The trail leads to Paris, involving Anna and her boyfriend Harry in a deepening conspiracy of gun-running and leftist revolution, all of it old hat and none of it very interesting. Anna tells her own story, but it just doesn't live up to her several forebodings of the "had I pub known" school of writing, a worn-out technique always used in vain to build up suspense. (F)*

Maxwell Grant, *Fingers of Death* (Jove V4279; c. 1933, 1960; 1st published in *The Shadow Magazine*, 1 March 1933; Jove/EBJ edition published September 1977; 144 pp.).

Pulp collectors know what prices that the original

magazines are selling for, so they can't help be pleased that Jove is continuing to bring out this series of paperback reprints, but it's also true that the early ones published so far are really pretty crude by today's standards. I can't help but wonder what market there is for them among mystery readers in general.

In this case The Shadow is as mysterious in his was as usual, but for the most part his presence in the murder-stricken town of Holmsford goes almost unnoticed as the prominent town leaders in on a 20-year-old conspiracy of crime do their best to wipe themselves out on their own. In this new version of the spoils system, it's the survivor who collects it all.

The cover by Steranko is very very striking, featuring as it does a particularly well-shaped damsel in distress, and it will do a lot in helping sales, as intended, but covers can't promote repeat business when the story is marred by what appears to be clumsy telling, and worse, repeats itself many times over--payment by the word, remember? (D)

Michael Collins, *The Blood-Red Dreams* (Dodd, Mead; c. 1976; 186 pp.).

New York City does not consist of Wall Street and Broadway and Times Square only. It consists of people, often living in ethnic proximity, many exiled from countries they remember only in dreams. Some try to change present dreams into reality, with the bitterness of forgotten heroes.

One-armed detective Dan Fortune, hired to find a girl's missing grandfather, finds himself involved in a new anti-Soviet militancy, nurtured chiefly among youth too young even to know the old country. Internal conflicts exist, motives have changed over the years, murder results.

Spoiling the basis for a fine tale with quite a different background is a slow-moving plot and leaden writing. Collins makes a number of pointed observations on target, but he can't seem to save this book from sinking because of its own weight. (C)

Ian Stuart Black, *The Man on the Bridge* (St. Martin's; c. 1975; 250 pp.).

The border between Albania and Greece, a bridge, a last desperate effort for escape. Failure, one dead, one survivor. Eighteen months in prison, then exchange back to England. Why then is British intelligence asking Munro to leave retirement in Eastbourne, to return to the scene of his nightmares, taking along a girl who says she's the dead man's wife?

Wheels within wheels. Everything seems to have two levels, two meanings. Just recently freed from the psychological pressure of his Albanian captors, not surprisingly Munro begins to question reality. He's both a cynic and a romantic, and maybe now he's paranoid. Nonetheless, he's trapped, no longer of free mind, in the controlled grip of his manipulators. This is a mind-racing suspense novel that will definitely swallow you up in the engulfing morass of eastern European intrigue. (A)

Jeffrey Ashford, *Slow Down the World* (Walker; c. 1976; 182 pp.).

Racing driver Jim Brice loses a fraction of his split-second reflexes in an accident, and shortly thereafter his career and his girl are gone. He drifts into a world of crime, but fate is kind enough to allow him to escape, on the run, behind a new identity.

Once underway the story may be faulted for predictability, but that's part of the secret of successful suspense writing--to write a story with believable characters and a couple of unusual twists but yet keeping the reader's mind aware of the dangers always just ahead. You won't put this one down right away. (A minus)

J. J. Marric, *Gideon's Drive* (Harper & Row; c. 1976; 166 pp).

If there is no Commander Gideon of Scotland Yard, there should be. He's head of the E.I.D., respected by both his men and the public at large, and represents the solid foundation of law and justice found in most segments of British life. Even though this is his last book, he's outlived his author, the late John Creasey, by several years, and one suspects that while we won't hear about it, he'll be responsible for the capture of many a criminal more, for the undoing of many a criminal plot still to come.

Here the plotters' plan is to take control of England's food supply, perhaps not as difficult as it sounds, what with supermarkets taking over the functions of the many specialist shops, shaving prices, forcing smaller competitors out of business. It's still just a little too fantastic and unconnected this time. Marric-Creasey shines more with the peripheral cases, neatly sketched in and combined as usual with domestic details, including those of Gideon's own family. (C plus)

Hugh Lamb, ed., *The Taste of Fear* (Taplinger; c. 1976; 1st published in the U.S., 1976; 237 pp.).

This may be a trifle out of place here, being a collection of obscure and never-before published ghost stories and other fantasies. Nor do I usually take the time to read this kind of story, or even try to.

The book's subtitle is "Thirteen Eerie Tales of Horror," which explains the intent, but the execution is abysmal. It may be me, but even a ghost story or fairy tale must have logical reason for happening, mustn't it?

One exception to the general run of what I found unreadable is a masterful tale by William Hope Hodgson, "From the Tideless Sea", about a man and a woman doomed to spend the rest of their lives on a ship trapped in the Sargasso Sea. The tragedy is compounded by the birth of a daughter, who will live out her short life in a world of true desolation and hopelessness, with unknown monsters lurking just below the seaweed. . . .

"Three Shall Meet" by Frederick Cowles is an atmospheric tale of an old mansion, a bitter hatred, and rats in a secret room. All the right ingredients. But as for the rest, if you're a fan of this sort of thing, take the rating below with some salt, but I'd suggest you're better off reading black-and-white comics like *Eerie* and *Creepy*. They have pictures too.

For the record, the other authors are: David Sutton, H. F. W. Tatham, Michael Sims, John Blackburn, E. H. Visiak, A. C. Benson, Ramsey Campbell, L. T. C. Rolt, Les Freeman, Erckmann-Chatrain, and Roger Parkes. (Overall rating: D)

June Drummond, *Slowly the Poison* (Walker & Co.,; c. 1975; first published in the U.S., 1976; 192 pp.).

"If a jury finds a man guilty, then everyone accepts the verdict, but if it finds him innocent, then doubt always lingers." In this case the verdict follows Hugh Frobisher's widow all the way to South Africa, where she goes by invitation to meet her husband's family.

The year is 1911, pre-World War I, in the sunny days of the British Empire. A leisurely time, but a compelling sotry. After facing the detailed inquiry of the coroner's inquest at Thameside, Alice builds her life anew, cautiously but coolly self-possessed. Then another attempt at murder; poison again. A very nice ending. (A)

Theodore Wilden, *To Die Elsewhere* (Harcourt Brace Jovanovich; c. 1976; translation of *Unrit nekde jinde*; 225 pp.).

A search for a missing CIA liaison agent in Marseilles turns into a race to obtain some stolen documents which reveal the truth behind President Kennedy's assassination. The intellectual approach--no suspense, and incredibly uninteresting. (F)

Bill Reade, *The Ibiza Syndicate* (St. Martin's; c. 1975; 172 pp.).

A self-retired civil servant on Ibiza finds himself recruited by MI6 when the island becomes the center of headline-making criminal activity. Being salvaged from the Mediterranean is a treasure-trove of precious Italian artwork once looted by the Nazis. Being blackmailed for a million pounds is the fictional equivalent of Aristotle Onassis.

It's all pretty unlikely, but it's fun while it lasts. Quick and slick James Bond stuff. (B minus)

Ray Grant Toepfer, *Endplay* (Fawcett Gold Medal M3200; c. 1975; 176 pp.).

A lot of paperbacks seem to sink without a trace soon after being published. Here's another. If it's out of print, as I would guess that it is, I wish you luck in finding this one.

Don't worry too much about it though. The book hits its peak about halfway through. After that the tension stops and the characters start thinking their way out of their predicament. Take the following quote, for example: "He replaced the phone and looked at it. It was moving now; the ball was rolling, and he had set it in motion. It could still be stopped of course. But he knew he didn't want to stop it. If Hardin knew where Carla was, it was a cinch McGowan wouldn't get it out of him. After all, it was Sam Hardin's life insurance, because as soon as he told McGowan

where, he'd be dead. But Hardin might tell Joey to save his
life, because he would have nothing to lose. Joe didn't
care where Carla was; he wouldn't kill Hardin for that. He
would ask Hardin where she was though, because Joey would
want to get McGowan in a position where McGowan would owe
him favors. Maybe."

McGowan is a cop, who falls in love with Carla, who has
run away from Hardin. Hardin is a crooked cop, working for
Joey, a minor underworld boss. That's about the story. It
begins very smoothly, with some interesting views from an
honest cop's end of things, but the long stretch of inaction
is too big a handicap to overcome. Above average, but stay
calm if you don't ever find a copy. (C plus)

David Alexander, *Die, Little Goose* (Bantam 1655; Random
House edition published April 1956; Bantam edition published
December 1957; 152 pp.).

Bart Hardin, hard-drinking and tough-gambling editor of
the *Broadway Times*, investigates murder in a theatrical
rooming house when his "secretary", an old actor kept on the
payroll for mostly sentimental reasons, is accused of killing a crippled dancer.

Times Square has changed considerably since the 1950s.
It still has the same bright lights and dark alleyways as
always, but the inhabitants are different. I think Bart
Hardin's world was a lot cleaner and far more decent. For
sophisticated Broadwayites, they sure can talk awfully
corny. Underneath, they must have hearts of gold.

The killer is easy to spot. Hardin knows on page 124,
and so should you. Only average, but a wave of nostalgia
for a vanished way of urban life may make it seem like more.
(C plus)

Robert Patrick Wilmot, *Blood in Your Eye* (Lippincott; c.
1952; 224 pp.).

America in the early 1950s was vexed with a praticularly noisome political affliction, one that occasionally shows
up even in private eye novels from that period, dating them
as badly as run-of-the-mill spy thrillers always seem to be.

Steve Considine is the detective in this one, an operative for a high-priced agency, the kind that's more than
willing to take a job like wet-nursing a society drunk trying to dry out. The guy's the sort of dedicated drinker who
sees things, however, and before they can get him to London
where an expensive doctor has a cure waiting, what he thinks
he sees is someone being murdered. To stay on his client's
trail, Considine is the sappy kind of dick who'll let himself be picked up and thrown into the same alcoholic ward;
he's also the kind of romantic who'll fall in love with the
girl involved at first sight, but it goes without saying
that even though he may stumble around for a while, he can
also be counted on to actually solve the case--all in a
day's work.

So where do the Commies come in? Look around, look
around. (C minus)

VERDICTS

(More Reviews)

Trevor Bernard, *Brightlight* (Manor Books, 1977, 204 pp.,$1½)
IMAGINARY COMPOSITE CONVERSATION
SCENE: OFFICES OF VARIOUS PUBLISHERS
   "Jeez! Not another detective book!"
   "Whatcha think bringin outa nu private jingle book, Ed?"
   "No chance! Those things got killed off in the Fifties when everybody was tryenna write like Mickey Spillane. Earlie Gardner and Halliday was about the oney ones survived. Either of 'em ever sends us an unsolicited book, you can bet you won't be first reader, kid."
   "Say, Charlie, think there's room for another Jewish detective series?"
   "Hardly! Why, there's kemelman's Rabbi, and . . . "
   "As well to say 'Lanigan's Rabbi' after that TV series, Charlie."
   "Yup. And Moses Wine, and then there's that odball one who always operates during World War II."
   "Think we could use a compassionate private eye, Chief?"
   "Nope. That fat one--the one sells steaks for Bonanza now--couldn't make it on TV."
   "Yeh, that's the one useta be Marshall Dillon on raido."
   "Reet."
   "Howabout this new 'eye' book. Drinks wine, the hero does?"
   "Shoo-oot, to coin a phrase, that went out with Mike Shayne, er was it Herky Poirot?"
   "Jeez! Not another detective manuscript!"
   With words not unlike the above, *Brightlight* must have progressed through the publisher's jungle that is New York City. Finally it made its way, like water through a Mr. Coffee, all the way down to Manor Books. Now, this decidedly minor publisher has given the public what may well be its first significant book. Their front cover blurb compares the author to "Hammett, Spillane, Chandler", and I, for one, don't find it too much of an exaggeration.
   Hero Nathan Brightlight is very nearly as down-and-out as most of the eyes we used to love during the Thirties, Forties and Fifites. He takes on, in this first case, a Hollywood mystery (shades of Prather, Don Rico, Nolan's Challis and others too numerous to mention!), but where most of those writers would have presented the story with a brittle flippancy, Trevor Bernard manages to make the reader care about his characters.
   An aging movie king's relatively new wife has disappeared, and Brightlight trails her through a maze of high (and very, very low) society, discovering a web of interlocking murders that would do credit to a Marlowe or a Harper [*Sic! and shame on you, Jeff Banks!*]. Finally, he covers up the last killing in the long series, in the interests of justice.
   Let's hope this isn't his last case!
   Read it, and if there's not another book about Bright-

light reasonably soon, you'll probably want to re-read it.
(R. Jeff Banks)

Robert B. Parker, *Mortal Stakes* (Houghton Mifflin, 1975, Berkley Medallion, 1977, 214 pp.).

If you like baseball, you'll like *Mortal Stakes*. If you don't like baseball, you should still like *Mortal Stakes*, particularly if you are now a "Spenser" fan (and so you should be), because *Mortal Stakes* has very little to do with baseball. *Mortal Stakes* is the third of Parker's "Spenser" series and immediately precedes the Edgar Award winning *Promised Land* (Houghton Mifflin, 1976).

Spenser's client in *Mortal Stakes* is a baseball general manager with a guilty conscience. As is typical of "Spenser", he ends up represented and tending to the interests of not necessarily his client, but the baseball club's star pitcher and his spouse with a background of questionable "practices". Along the way, "Spenser", the hottest detective since Lew Archer, manages to uncover elements of blackmail, prostitution and murder.

Again, Mr. Parker thoroughly entertains his readers with a delightful character, who every mother should love in spite of his philosophy towards marriage and his very unorthodox manner of making a living. "Spenser", however, portrays a social critic, gourmet cook, physical fitness freak, sculptor and unabashed participant in the abnormal scheme of things to the degree of excellence and irresistibility.

The only problem you might have with *Mortal Stakes* is if you have already read *Promised Land*, which is the best Parker to date. *Mortal Stakes* is good, however, and considered by this reviewer to be highly worthwhile reading in the (hopefully) continuing saga of "Spenser", Boston's premier private investigator. (Larry L. French)

H.R.F. Keating, ed., *Agatha Christie: First Lady of Crime* (Holt, Rinehart and Winston, 1977, 224 pp., $12.95).

Agatha Christie, who died last year at the age of 85, remains a phenomenon.

Her detective novels are still enormous best sellers in numerous languages, topped only by the Bible and Shakespeare. Her melodrama "The Mousetrap" is still running successfully in London since 1952, the longest running play in world theatre history. Following the stellar "Murder on the Orient Express", additional motion pictures based on her stories are now planned, the first one being "Death on the Nile", to be filmed in Egypt.

And a growing number of studies about Dame Agatha and her literary input have been published recently, testifying to her undiminished popularity.

H.R.F. Keating, crime critic for *The London Times* and author of the series of detective novels featuring Inspector Ghote of the Bombay C.I.D., has assembled some luminary practitioners in the field of suspense fiction, and they have put forward a combined look at the "first lady of crime."

Elizabeth Walker, a distinguished writer of the supernatural, relates the Case of the Escalating Sales. Christie's first novel, *The Mysterious Affair at Styles* (1920), introducing a diminuative Belgian detective named Hercule Poirot, was rejected by several publishers, eventually accepted for publication, paying its author 125 dollars, selling a mere 2,000 copies. Gradually her books became increasingly popular, were translated into more than one hundred languages and to date their sales have exceeded 400 million copies.

Julian Symons, award winning author of crime novels, analyses Christie's works, concentrating mainly on her masterpieces *And Then There Were None, The Murder of Roger Ackroyd* and *The ABC Murders*. He theorizes that her chances of survival as an author who will be read a century from now are good, not because "she was a great or even a good writer" but "because she was the supreme mistress of a magical skill that is a permanent concern of humanity: the construction and the solution of puzzles."

Edmund Crispin, who has written eight detective stories which have given him a secure place in the annals of the genre, hails Agatha Christie's knack for simple plotting, solid construction, variety in her prose style and realism of English country life.

Michael Gilbert, the prolific author, reveals interesting details of Agatha's personal life: a shy, private girl who was provoked into writing by some remark made by her sister; an impending breakup of her marriage that caused her to suffer amnesia and disappear for a while, a highly controversial event that was blown out of proportion by the press; a vacation trip to Baghdad, where she met her second husband, a distinguished archaeologist; the war years during which she produced twelve complete novels while working long hours as a nurse in a hospital; eventual acclaim that brought her a fortune and honors, yet did not change a very private way of life.

Emma Lathan, author of many highly praised mystery novels notable for their solid background of the business world, explains the reasons for Christie's success in America: a fascination with a never-never land where voices are rarely raised, where breeding is more important than money; the humour is universal; there are fleeting vignettes constituting an irresistable interpretation of the human condition.

Half a dozen romances, written by Agatha Christie under the pseudonym Mary Westmacott, are evaluated by Dorothy B. Hughes, a superb suspense novelist and critic. She claims that these unheralded works encompass some of the best of Christie's writing, are in fact a fictionalized autobiography and collectively project an affirmation of life.

Then there are two excellent articles about Christie's achievements on the stage (notably "The Little Indians", "The Mousetrap", "Witness for the Prosecution", "Spider's Web") and the silver screen (mainly the series of comedy-thrillers featuring Margaret Rutherford, the first version of *And Then There Were None* directed by Rene Clair, "Witness for the Prosecution" starring Charles Laughton, Marlene Dietrich and Tyrone Power and the recent "Murder on the Orient Express).

Sadly lacking is a chapter about Christie's fascinating series detectives: Tommy and Tupence Beresford, with a nose for adventure; Superintendent Battle, who proved that not all literary policemen were bumbling foils for the amateur detective; Parker Pyne, who always made good his assurance to make his clients happy; and Harly Quin who possessed a supernatural aura.

But the anthology culminates with two portraits of Christie's most celebrated super-sleuths: Hercule Poirot, the eccentric Belgian with the egg-shaped head and waxed moustache, whose "little grey cells" were the nemesis of clever criminals for over half a century; and Jane Marple, the tall, elderly spinster who is prone to gossip and whose uncanny gift to fathom human nature was an important tool in her indefatigable investigative career.

Numerous illustrations highlight many aspects of Agatha Christie's private and public life.

Altogether, a respectable, penetrating and affectionate tribute to a writer who perhaps gave more pleasure to more people than any other single contemporary. (Amnon Kabatchnik)

Elleston Trevor, *The Theta Syndrome* (Doubleday, 1977, 233 pp., $7.95).

Elleston Trevor, a prolific author of detective, adventure and espionage fiction, has written now a modern horror tale.

Claudia Terman is a victim of an unexplained freeway crash. She is lying in a hospital room, her brain functioning feebly, in the theta-rhythm range, the twilight zone of consciousness.

Then odd things began to happen in the hospital: a nurse experiencing periodic seizures in which her hand involuntarily penned frantic messages for help . . . a tray of instruments crashing to the floor . . . a brain surgeon in the operating room taking up a scalpel and then sagging to the floor, dying.

Finally it became evident that somebody was coming to finish the job that the rigged accident had started. It would be so easy: Just pull out the plug of Claudia's breathing machine. Who was coming? The girl's aggressive husband? Drunken brother? Shy Admirer? Crooked employer? The only clue to a killer's identity was the silent scream of a terrified brain.

The theme dangles on a thin line of credulity, but the author manages to capture interest by conveying a realistic atmosphere of the intricate routine in the Intensive Care Unit of a hospital and by presenting identifyable characters. The pace is furious and there is a steady build-up towards a suspenseful climax, even though one wishes for an additional plot twist before the end.

Elleston Trevor is best known for his spy thrillers, which he writes under the pseudonym "Adam Hall". *The Quiller Memorandum* (1965) won the Edgar by the Mystery Writers of America and the French Grand Prix de Literature Policiere. It was made into a successful movie starring George Segal and Alec Guiness, and was followed by a string of novels featuring the same double-agent. (Arnon Kabatchnik)

Basil Copper, *The Curse of the Fleers* (St. Martin's, 1977, 140 pp., $7.95).
The latest chilling macabre mystery by Basil Copper is an old fashioned Gothic thriller penned grandly, unblushingly, with very little subtlety and lots of melodrama.
The elderly Sir John Fleer is driven to the very brink of madness when an ancient family curse returns to haunt him. A hideous apparition lurks in the eerie battlements and labyrinthine passageways of his ancestral home.
Soon a treacherous web of deadly intrigue surrounds the noble family. Three horrifying murders occur. Secret passages are discovered. A hidden fortune in gold may be the cause for all the sordid deeds. A celebrated master of disguise and a grotesque menagerie, containing a giant ape, are part of the nightmarish proceedings. Torture instruments that can compete with any devices invented by Edgar Allan Poe play a major role in the climactic sequences.
The family curse, the secluded manor, the diabolical villain and the courageous hero were originated and cultivated in the 18th century by such master story tellers as "Monk" Lewis, Ann Radcliffe and Mary Shelley. Basil Copper proves that the same ingredients, treated with stylish gusto, can still be gripping and enjoyable today. (Arnon Kabatchnik)

Elmore Leonard, *The Hunted* (Dell, 1977, $1.75).
Al Rosen is hiding in Israel, after accepting immunity for testifying against two gangsters in the United States. He receives a large, monthly payment every month from his former company, the money being delivered by a marine on duty at the United States Embassy. Rosen has a pleasant life, no money worries and an occasional affair with women from charter tours.
Inevitably, this comes to an end, when the gangsters trace Rosen to Israel and send three hit men to kill him. From here on the story is repetitious; the gangsters locate Rosen, lose him, then find him again until they finally catch up with him in the last chapters. The marine includes himself in the fight to save Rosen, simply because he is bored, using his experience in Korea to baffle the gangsters.
The reader is apt to become as bored as the marine; there is not one interesting characterization in this book, no mystery and no suspense because no one will care what happens to Al Rosen anyway. (Myrtis Broset)

Ben Bova, *The Multiple Man* (Ballantine Books, 1977, $1.75).
Science fiction stories usually take place in the future with all the fantastic inventions science promises. This book has all this but it has more. It is a fine mystery with breath-taking suspense. As James Halliday, President of the United States, is speaking in Boston, a dead man, looking exactly like the President, is found in an alley. The Secret Service takes over to try to keep this

quiet and Press Secretary Meric Albano is warned not to tell anyone. When the Chief of the Secret Service lets slip that another dead man was found in Denver, he too the President's twin, Albano, who admires and respects the man he works for, is afraid that someone wants to assassinate the President and substitute his own man. Albano begins to question people and examine records with the help of his female assistant and a Secret Service agent. When the President's bodyguard, along with a scientist, is killed in a plane crash, Albano suspects murder. Meric travels to Colorado to talk to General Halliday, the President's father, where he is threatened and again warned to keep quiet.

Who are the dead men who resemble the President so closely? Is the General trying to get rid of his own son? Is the President's wife involved? These are the questions Albano means to find answers to, and he is determined to keep on with his investigation, though terrified for himself and his assistant.

If this is to be your first science fiction book, be sure and read it, you won't want to put it down until you reach the last word. (Myrtis Broset)

F. H. Hall, *The Lamb White Days* (Pocket Books, 1977, $1.50).

When Cricket Crane, ex-reporter turned antique dealer, pulls Tommy Kinsella out of Lake Michigan he believes a call to the Coast Guard will be all that is necessary to return Tommy to his family. Robert Kinsella tells Cricket to keep the boy for the present and he will send money for expenses, leaving Cricket in a highly puzzled state.

Tommy settles in satisfactorily with the Crane family, consisting of Cricket, his wife Polly and daughter Flip, who adores Tommy. When the body of Tommy's mother is washed ashore and Kinsella arrested for murder, there is no question of the boy remaining with the Cranes. Cricket soon begins to think of Tommy as a son but Flip loses her liking for Tommy and Polly advises Cricket to pay more attention to his daughter and not to become entangled with the Kinsellas, a failing of Cricket's which causes him to lose his job with the newspaper, because he invariably became involved with the people he wrote about.

Cricket's nature being what it is, he is unable to regard Tommy objectively. When Tommy asks to see his stepsister, who is living with her grandparents, Cricket takes him to visit only to be told by the grandmother that they want nothing to do with the Kinsellas. Cricket meets a young man and a girl, both employed by Tommy's grandparents, who offer to help Cricket, claiming Kinsella is crooked.

Their investigations into Kinsella's life get them into trouble with F.B.I. agents, who are not pleased with this meddling. When a private detective, who had been following Crane, is murdered, the F.B.I. men become suspicious of Crane and his friends, and Cricket finds himself getting deeper in a situation he does not understand.

The give-and-take between Cricket and Polly, a most understanding wife, add humor to a story of blackmail and murder. An immensely enjoyable book. (Myrtis Broset)

Lucinda Blair, *The Place of Devils* (Berkley, 1977, $1.75).

This story takes place in the year 1879, in an era when women of twenty-three were regarded as spinsters, already being too old for men to want to marry them.

It is partly for this reason and also because she is attracted to the man, that Lalie Cortland accepts the offer of marriage from Rafael de Casta, who is looking for a mother for his small daughter Carmen.

Carmen's mother was a Navajo whom De Casta married, knowing that the Government disapproved of mixed marriages. De Casta's wife, loving her husband, ran away when she feared De Casta would lose his trader's license because of the marriage. De Casta finds some bones and his wife's wedding ring in the desert; believing she must be dead he buries the bones and places a marker inscribed simply "Cata" over the grave.

Lalie's attraction for De Casta turns into love but he shows no affection for her, regarding her as his daughter's governess. Carmen insists her mother comes to visit her at night and when Lalie sees a woman leaving the house one night she believes Cata is still alive and that De Casta is in contact with her. Lalie is attacked in the house and her fear of Cata grows. When a friend of Lalie's is found murdered, wearing a cape of Lalie's, Lalie believes Cata killed the girl thinking it was Lalie.

This is an innocuous story written for the Gothic trade who will identify with Lalie. (Myrtis Broset)

Ngaio Marsh, *Death in Ecstasy* (Berkley, 1977, $1.50).

The House of the Sacred Flame is located on a small street in London and presided over by Jasper Garnette, founder and priest of the temple. From the congregation, seven people have been chosen for the inner circle, all devoted to Garnette and contributors to his cause.

On a Sunday night the Inner Circle gathers with its priest for a special ceremony. The sacred cup filled with wine is passed from hand to hand, Cara Quayne drinks, gasps violently and drops dead.

Newsman Nigel Bathgate, an observer at the ritual, calls his friend Roger [sic] Alleyn, Chief Inspector at Scotland Yard. Alleyn arrives with his assistant Fox; they note there is enmity among the members of the Circle, and dislike for the two homosexuals who serve as acolytes to Garnette. Upon questioning, Alleyn learns that Cara was in love with Garnette, another woman in the Circle was intensely jealous. A young man is found under the influence of drugs, his fiancee has joined the Circle to protect him. Alleyn wonders why an American business man is found in this strange company.

Alleyn and Fox uncover a theft and the source of drugs while looking for a murderer. This is one of Marsh's earliest books, also one of her best. The dialogue is bright and often witty, the story has a tortuous plot and moves speedily along. (Myrtis Broset)

Trevor Bernard, *Brightlight* (Manor Books, 1977, $1.50).

Nathan Brightlight is hired by Derek Flanders, whose

wife has disappeared. As Brightlight roves the California coast and through the film studios he discovers there is much about the woman no one is telling him. Why doesn't Flanders mention his wife had a previous marriage? Who is the drug addict A-ne Flanders visits at the hospital? Why did Anne disappear immediately after a hit-and-run accident in which a man and girl were killed? Did Anne Flanders know about her husband's affairs with other women?

The story has an animated beginning, but after a few chapters the author let the plot drift and then tried to rescue it in the last chapter. The solution to Ann's disappearance become apparent half-way through the book.

Bernard is advertised as a successor to Hammett and Chandler on the book's cover but this story does not have the impact of any book written by either of these two authors. (Myrtis Broset)

Ngaio Marsh, *Scales of Justice* (Berkley, 1977, $1.50).

A quiet English village where a secret has been kept for many years. When old Sir Harold Lacklander knows he is dying he decides to reveal the secret and sends his memoirs to a neighbor, Colonel Cartarette. Cartarette, astounded and unhappy after reading the papers, nevertheless feels they should be made public to remedy an injustice done years ago. The Colonel makes his intentions known and is found murdered beside a stream where he has been fishing.

When Scotland Yard is called, Chief Inspector Alleyn, with his assistant Fox, is sent to the village. Alleyn is told by Sir Harold's wife, a strong, dominating woman, that she was talking to Cartarette just before the murder but refuses to tell the subject of the conversation. Sir Harold's son and the Colonel's wife state that they were playing golf together, both deny any interest in each other and claim they did not see Cartarette at the stream. Dr. Mark Lacklander and the Colonel's daughter are obviously in love with each other but something unknown is tearing them apart. Cartarette has an alcoholic neighbor who does not reveal to the police he was a former lover of the Colonel's wife. There is another neighbor, an eccentric widower who lives alone with his cats and quarrels with the others in the neighborhood.

It is among this group that Alleyn seeks for the murderer; his task is made difficult by all these people refusing information. The book is a little heavy reading in parts of it, but Marsh does her usual g-od job in developing a plot and bringing her story to a logical climax. (Myrtis Broset)

Len Deighton, *The Billion Dollar Brain* (Berkley, 1977,$1.95)

A British intelligence agent who remains nameless throughout the book, but uses the name Liam Dempsey, is sent to Finland where he meets Harvey Newbegin, a U. S. agent. Dempsey does not trust Harvey but they make plans to work together to keep the Russians from obtaining the formula for keeping viruses alive in eggs.

Harvey sends a case of empty eggs to Russia by another agent; Dempsey follows, only to be captured by the K.G.B.

He is released under circumstances that make it look as though he has betrayed the other man. Dempsey scents the artful hand of Newbegin in this action. Could it be revenge because Dempsey made love to Harvey's mistress?

The scene moves to New York then on to Texas where Harvey and the girl both show up again. The computer called The Brain is located in Houston--The Brain correlates all intelligence reports and gives orders--which Dempsey ignores as he considers it ridiculous to be speaking to a computer. Harvey decides to leave his family and defect to Russia with the eggs containing the live viruses, this means Dempsey must follow.

Deighton does not write the traditional spy story, there are none of the torture episodes and killings between agents that are usually found; the characters are unconsciously humorous, his hero moves swiftly and lightly but effectively. An ingenious book. (Myrtis Broset)

Len Deighton, *An Expensive Place to Die* (Berkley, 1977, $1.4).
Deighton's nameless agent is back, this time in France, though it is not clear why he is there since the matters he becomes involved in usually come under the jurisdiction of the police.

A police officer, who uses his ex-wife and a prostitute as informers, together with the un-named agent, try to solve a murder case and uncover the mystery of a clinic run by a self-styled psychiatrist. The answers are not concealed from the reader.

This is not a spy story, the only intelligence work being done is retained until the last chapter. It is not as intricately plotted as Deighton's other books--the idea of the story being buried under the relations between the characters.

For no one except ardent Deighton fans. (Myrtis Broset)

Evelyn Anthony, *The Rendezvous* (Berkley, 1977, $1.95).
When Terese Bradford and Karl Amstat meet at a New York party, it is the beginning of a new life for Terese and the ending of an old one for Amstat, a former Nazi officer, who has changed his name from Alfred Brunnerman to his new identity.

Terese, a French underground worker during the war, was captured and tortured by the Gestapo and subsequently spent ten months in Buchenwald. She was rescued by the arrival of the American army led by Bob Bradford, who later married Terese, then had the memory of her ordeal erased from her mind, through hypnotism, by army psychiatrist Dr. Joe Kaplan.

Terese naturally does not connect Amstat with the Nazi Brunnerman who interrogated her during the war. She and Karl fall in love and proceed to have an affair though Karl realizes his whole world will collapse should Terese regain her memory.

Dr. Kaplan, now in New York, and a friend of the Bradfords, becomes suspicious of Amstat and passes his suspicion on to the Israeli execution squad, who have been searching for Brunnerman. While the Israelis are backtracking on Amstat, seeking a clue that he is Brunnerman, Karl receives a warning phone call and makes plans to leave the country. Terese, desperately in love with Karl by now, leaves Bradford and goes along with Amstat. The couple try to hide their trail, with the Isarelis ever getting closer, with the intention of killing Karl, when they locate him.

The reader will waver between sympathy for the ill-matched lovers and horror at the revelations of Karl's past. Principally a love story but with enough suspense to make a vastly entertaining book. (Myrtis Broset)

Ngaio Marsh, *Death at the Bar* (Berkley, 1977, $1.50).

Three friends, a painter, an actor and a lawyer gather at a village inn; the lawyer never leaves. When these three meet with the local people at the inn's pub for a friendly dart game, the lawyer, Luke Watchman, volunteers for a trick exhibition put on by Bob Legge, an expert with the darts. As Watchman spreads his hand and Legge throws the darts which are intended to land between the fingers, one misses and hits Watchman in the finger. Watchman, frightened at the sight of blood, collapses whereupon Decima Moore, a bystander, offers him a glass of brandy; Watchman gasps the word "poison"—the lights go out, and when they come on again, Watchman is dead.

A doctor is called, his diagnosis is death by cyanide poisoning and, indeed, cyanide is found on the dart that struck Watchman. The others in the pub all swear that Legge could not have poisoned the dart since they were watching him all the time, thus leading to the proprietor, Abel Pomeroy, being blamed for his carelessness with the rat poison he has been using. In his distress Pomeroy goes to Scotland Yard Inspector Alleyn who is interested but cannot take any action unless asked to do so by the local police. However, Alleyn does write a letter to the village officials who are only too hapy to have Scotland Yard investigate the matter since they suspect murder but cannot prove anything.

Alleyn and his assistant Fox go to the village where they find plenty of suspects with motives, but no opportunity for anyone to commit murder. None of the people in the pub were in a position to poison the dart and there is no trace of poison in the bottle of brandy or the glass used by Decima Moore when she offered the brandy to Watchman. After questioning Alleyn discovers Watchman's two friends inherit his money, Decima had been overheared in a quarrel with the murdered man, the proprietor's son who was friendly with Legge, disliked Watchman, and Legge himself had been taunted by Watchman for an unknown reason. Is one of these people guilty of murder or was the death accidnetal?

A plot that moves logically, that twists and turns and keeps the reader guessing until the solution is divulged by Alleyn in the final chapter, makes this an unusual mystery and one that is up to Marsh's standard. (Myrtis Broset)

Andrew Patrick, *Baretta* (Berkley, 1977, $1.50).

High-powered drugs are coming into the city and the Los Angeles Police Department is out to find the dealers. The action is all centered on Tony Baretta but it is extremely doubtful that any police force in the country allows its officers to behave in the manner of Baretta.

There isn't much of a plot as we are told early in the book the names of the narcotics dealers and it is a certainty that Baretta will catch up to them. Baretta does not shine as a detective; as a police officer he is absurd.

The only mystery to this book is why it was ever published. (Myrtis Broset)

Dorothy Uhnak, *The Investigation* [*No publisher or date, Jane?--ed.*]

Joe Peters, protagonist of Dorothy Uhnak's *The Investigation*, is a cop with a lot going for--and against--him. Working in his behalf are his skills at his job, his dedication to it, the favors owed him by colleagues, and the interest and clout of his lifelong friend and superior officer, Tim Neary. Working against him are his pending retirement, his troubled marriage, and the political ambitions and departmental power of that same Tim Neary.

These factors provide the subplots of the book, dealing with intradepartmental spies, a race for mayoral nomination, and the Joe-and-Jan Peters midlife crisis. Against them, is plaid out the central story line of Peters' investigation of the murder of two little boys, the sons of Kitty and George Keeler. The crime itself is horrible, but its sensationalism is multiplied by Kitty Keeler's reputation. A stunningly beautiful blond wearing a tough-guy mask, Kitty is an intriguing character. Her own mother perceives her as a monster, selfish and wicked; yet, an elderly neighbor finds her loving--more tender and loyal than the woman's own children. Reputed to be sleeping around, Kitty is described by a battery of male acquaintances as a truly straight, sound friend, and chief among her supporters is her husband. Peters takes to the mean streets to solve the double murder and the puzzle of Kitty's personality.

Up and down those mean streets, Peters and the reader encounter a huge range of characters: political kingmakers, the guys at headquarters, the Queens District Attorney (and his staff and spies), George's employees, Kitty's family, and at least a third of the local underworld, most of them Kitty's loyal lads. Here, the cops out-tough the crooks and loyalty seems to flourish more among the hoods than among the good guys. Some of these portraits, however, are neatly done characterizations: George Keeler, his bartender Danny Fitzmartin, and "The Madonna of Forest Hills Gardens", for instance. From these characterizations stem some sound and effective scenes: a bitter exchange between Kitty and her mother, a moment between Danny and Lucille Traverna just after a death, and the parking lot meet between Peters and Benjamin the Cuban.

These strong portraits and sharp scenes contribute effectively to the tension in the book. *The Investigation* is an interesting novel whose large cast functions effectively as background and, in a sense, to provide local color. Their use in explication is genuinely well handled. The book reads well and holds the reader's interest--almost despite Joe Peters and Kitty Keeler. These two, regardless of Uhnak's obvious efforts, are not so effective--we have met them, under other names, before. (Jane S. Bakerman)

George C. Chesbro, *Shadow of a Broken Man* (Simon & Schuster, 1977).
 Most first novels are clumsy affairs.
 Chesbro's is no exception. The problem is one of indecision. Chesbro decides to write a detective novel. All the good detectives are all ready taken: Holmes (thin and tall), Wolfe (short and fat), etc. So Chesbro decides to make his detective a freak.
 Dr. Robert (Mongo) Frederickson is a dwarf.
 And, like so many First Novels, Chesbro makes the mistake of trying to put too much into it. He has his dwarf detective saving the Free World.
 On the plus side, Chesbro is an ad-quate writer, not Raymond Chandler <u>incarnate</u> as the advance praise printed on the dustjacket would have you believe. But Chesbro's writing skills are lost in the bewildering blend of spies and diplomats falling out of windows.
 And finally, the introduction of a true Telepath is just going too far. Any astute reader should be able to identify the hidden Telepath about halfway through the book.
 Chesbro's problem is that he doesn't know whether he is writing science fiction or suspense literature. The character of a dwarf is not explored, except for some blunt insults. Chesbro should have interviewed some dwarfs to find out what's it really like and reflected that in his character. As it is, the character could have been a woman or a black or any other minority for all the impact it had on the plot. (George Kelley)

Max Collins, *The Slasher* (Berkley, 1977).
 Not long ago I reviewed the other Max Collins, including the previous three Quarry novels. *The Slasher* breaks no new ground.
 Quarry continues the awkward role of being the hit man's hit man (that is, killing the professional hit man before he can kill his victim). This time the victim is a porno movie maker.
 I keep coming back to Collins' characters, Noland and Quarry, as spin-off's of Richard Stark/Donald Westlake's Parker.
 There's the same attempt to portray a world of complete amorality. But Collins is not successful. The reason is that Collins' characters aren't as smart as Parker is.
 Parker doesn't kill people stupidly, as Quarry does; Parker kills only when he has to, and that is a virtue. Quarry kills all the time, making it look too easy. There doesn't seem to be any serious complications in Quarry's deathtrip. And without complications, things get boring.
 Collins has some narrative powers. What he needs is a good editor, or failing that, a good self-examination of his work in terms of plot and character. Maybe a re-reading of the Parker books would help.
 The point is, Collins' series isn't going anywhere, isn't developing and isn't worth your time. (George Kelley)

Edmund Crispin, *The Moving Toyshop* (Penguin Books, 1977, 205 pp.; first published in 1946).

Cadogan, a major British poet, stumbles over a corpse in a dusty room above an Oxford toyshop. Next morning, Cadogan and Professor Gervase Fen return to the scene only to find that the corpse has vanished, as well as the toyshop. For the rest of the day and into the evening, they dash about Oxford searching for the corpse, the toyshop, the motive for the murder, and the murderer, at times accompanied by some or all of a beautiful shop girl, an ancient university don, a lorry driver, and one or more undergraduates. The reader is left quite breathless. Some of Fen's methods are of doubtful legality, but they lead to the desired results. By the end of an exhausting day they have uncovered the toyshop, the motive, the murderer, and almost incidentally the body of the unfortunate victim. This is a welcome reprinting of a light and sometimes exciting modern classic of murder and adventure. Highly recommended. (Paul McCarthy)

Julian Symons, *The Man Who Lost His Wife* (Penguin Books, 1977, 204 pp.; first published in 1970).

Although it is published as a Penguin CRIME book, this is very much a straight novel. A publisher travels from London to Yugoslavia in search of his second wife, her whereabouts providing the only element of mystery in the story. The character of the publisher is developed in a series of episodes involving his first wife, his colleagues and the authors of the publishing house, and casual acquaintances (male and female) in Yugoslavia. All ends well--perhaps: Symons quite effectively leaves the reader in doubt. The reader who expects a crime story the equal of *The Progress of a Crime* or *The Colour of Murder* or *The End of Soloman Grundy* will be disappointed. However, read without prejudice, *The Man Who Lost His Wife* comes across as a fine tale of adventure and an interesting study of character. It is a must for all true fans of Julian Simons. (Paul McCarthy)

Masterpieces of Mystery (Davis Publications, Inc.).

This is a continuing series, begun in 1976, of beautifully bound and relatively inexpensive collections of short stories, selected by Ellery Queen. Each volume has a theme of its own. *The Supersleuths* contains stories featuring the leading fictional detectives; the authors of the stories in *The Prizewinners* have won Nobel or Pulitzer prizes; the stories in *The Grand Masters* are by recipients of that honor; *The Golden Age*, Parts I and II, feature stories by authors from that period; the stories in *Detective Directory--I*, were chosen for the occupation of their authors, such as doctor, lawyer, teacher, and artist. Virtually all of the great authors and great detectives are represented by at least one story, and some by several. Each volume contains remarks by Ellery Queen on the theme of the volume, and at the beginning of each story is a picture of the author with a short biographical sketch. All things considered, it is a very attractive series. (Paul McCarthy)

Stuart Kaminsky, *Bullet for a Star* (St. Martins, 1977, 188pp)

If you've enjoyed the Hollywood-based detective novels of Andrew Bergman (*The Big Kiss-Off of 1944* or *Hollywood and LeVine*) done in the Hammett-Chandler tradition, then pick up a copy of this book.

Time: 1940. Place: Hollywood. Detective: Toby Peters. Peters, a private investigator, but former security officer for Warner Brothers, is hired by producer Sid Adelman to protect their new "star", Errol Flynn, from being blackmailed and possibly murdered. It seems that someone has taken some compromising pictures of the star with a very young girl. Flynn claims they are fake. Peters' job is to deliver $5,000 in return for the negative and one print, so the studio can determine whether the picture is for real or not.

Kaminsky, a professor at Northwestern University, uses his knowledge of the movie industry with great skill as he takes us behind the scenes and on the back lots of Warner Brothers to find the blackmailer. With the help of the likes of Humphrey Bogart and Peter Lorre, two other promising stars, Peters succeeds, but not before finding three dead bodies and being sent to the hospital twice. (James Jobst)

Robert Pollock, *Loophole: Or How to Rob a Bank* (Fawcett, 1975; E. P. Dutton, 1973; 191 pp.).

After seeing the great reviews on the cover of this book, I was very disappointed after finishing it. I enjoy "caper" books, but this one left me flat. I don't know what else Robert Pollock has written, but this one isn't worth the effort. The whole time I was reading this book, I was thinking just how much better Donald E. Westlake does this sort of thing. His characters are always funny, likeable, and we are sympathetic towards them. We want them to succeed. They are crooks, but "nice" crooks.

The two main characters, Mike Daniels, a professional safecracker, and Stephen Booker, an unemployed architect, team up to "rob a bank" in London. Pollock's attempt at making the characters "heroes" or even "anti-heroes" fails. At the end of the book we aren't really interested in finding out whether Daniels and Booker are going to be successful or not. They are. But who cares? (James Jobst)

Gerald Seymour, *Harry's Game* (Fawcett, 1975; Random House, 1975; 303 pp.).

I saw in the July TAD that Seymour's *The Glory Boys* was nominated for Best Novel of 1976, so I decided to pick up *Harry's Game* (his first), since *The Glory Boys* isn't available in paperback yet. It is definitely worth reading particularly if you are interested in what is going on in Northern Ireland at the present time.

The "Harry" in the title is Captain Harry James Brown, a secret agent and general troubleshooter for Her Majesty's Government. After Henry Danby, the Secretary of State for the Social Services, is gunned down in front of his house in view of his wife and children, Harry is sent into Belfast to find "The Man" who did it. He is suspected to be a member of the Provisional IRA, but a special one; a "loner" who is not known by most of the members, but only used on special jobs like assassinations. For Capt. Harry Brown in the guise of expatirate "Harry McEvoy" the job proves quite demanding.

Seymour does a fine job of showing us how both sides, the Special Patrol Group and the Provisional IRA, operate. The two main characters are developed quite well in the story. We learn about Harry's background, his family, and his opinions about his homeland and its people. We see Billy Downs, the man Harry is chasing, with his wife and children, and among his fellow members of the IRA. At the end of the book we become empathetic towards both men and the different lives they lead. (James Jobst)

Tony Kendrick, *Stealing Lillian* (Warner Books, 1975; PB edition, 1976; 279 pp.).

Bunny Calder is a small-time con artist working his magic charm and Robert Redford looks in New York City. He works for the Haverstraw Travel Agency during the day, and on long greakfast-, coffee-, and lunch-breaks he runs his own employment agency in the building next door. The fun begins when Ella Brown, an interior decorator for Bloomingdale's Department Store, stops in at the travel agency to inquire about taking a short vacation in the Caribbean. Not only is Bunny successful in selling her a vacation, but he also manages to get wax impressions of the keys to her beautiful apartment. He uses these to rent Ella's apartment, without her knowledge or permission, to a couple from Ohio who are visiting the Big Apple during the same time that Ella is going to be in the Caribbean. The plan fails, however, when the nice couple from Ohio, along with some of their friends, decide to play football in Ella's *House & Garden* apartment. The result: $7,000 worth of damages. Ella goes to her lawyer, Herb Smathers, who in turn gets in touch with the Immigration Department. They don't deport Bunny, but in order to make restitution for the damages to Ella's apartment, they persuade (blackmail) Bunny into helping the Immigration Department catch four terrorists who have come into the country illegally and who are looking for a quick way to raise twenty million dollars to buy a fighter bomber.

The con is finally set up with Bunny and Ella playing a multimillionaire couple, Don Ray and Jane Bergstrom, with loving daughter, Sherrel Ann. Sherrel Ann, being played by a foul-mouthed, fast-talking orphan named Lillian.

From the back cover of this book we learn that Tony Kendrick is an Australian who has written quite a number (how many it doesn't say) of books, and that three of them—*A Tough One to Lose*, *Seven Day Soldiers*, and this one—are going to be made into movies. After finishing *Stealing Lillian*, I certainly would like to see the movie version of it. If you enjoy Donald E. Westlake and his comic-mysteries, then you will enjoy Tony Kendrick and *Stealing Lillian*. (James Jobst)

J. S. LeFanu, *Uncle Silas; A Tale of Bartram-Haugh*, Introduction by Frederick Shroyer (Dover, 1966, $4.00).

I have been given the task of setting my thoughts concerning *Uncle Silas* on paper for the readers of *The Mystery Fancier*. Some would perhaps shrink from the assignment of reading the perils faced by a young girl in Victorian England, but not I. Sheridan Le Fanu's rather lengthy novel is a classic in the field of gothic horror and I felt a book to be read.

But there are problems faced by reviewing such a well-touted and recognized piece of fiction--one is told repeatedly that the story is horrific, or suspenseful or terrifying, so much so that the level of expectancy is rather high.

Briefly, *Uncle Silas* involves a few years in the life of Maud Ruthyn, a young heiress who at the tender and impressionable age of 17 is sent to live with her notorious Uncle Silas until legal age. Uncle Silas has no money; Maud has riches, and upon her death her vast sums are to be inherited by her uncle.

Culturally, the book is quite interesting; we are given a world filled with outdated customes, fashions and vehicles. The story is told by Maud in a style that is rather proper, since she is a *very* refined young lady and the style itself, is one seldom encountered in modern day detective fiction; it possesses a diarylike and genteel tone in narrative. Much of the book, however, is conversational and it is here that much of the feeling of the era emerges. Such scenes as Maud trying to teach the fineries of life to Silas's unschooled daughter Millie (the two girls become good friends); Millie and Maud visiting their cousin Lady Monica, or meeting up with the workers that live on the estate clearly demonstrate the class consciousness of the decade. It should be stressed that *Uncle Silas* is far from a heavy novel. Pages of long lengthy narrative seldom occur and although the book is intended as a drama, bright and humorous episodes occur intermittently.

But, here I have said nothing of the suspense! True, the wicked characters--the morbid evil governess Madame de la Rougierre, the ghostlike Uncle Silas, and his treacherous son Dudley--are not pleasant, but I did not find the atmosphere of "unrelenting suspense" for which the story is most noted. One knows Maud is in danger, but the terror is discreet and not horrifying. It is not until the last thirty pages, that the tempo truly accelerates and one is faced with horrible and mysterious scenes.

Perhaps it was I who was at fault and the true flavor of *Uncle Silas* is better experienced by a reading in one or two sittings and not many days. The continuity of the story is then fully captured, but this theory is most probably at fault as the novel itself was originally presented in installation form.

I do not mean to deny the worth of *Uncle Silas*--the characters both good and evil are interesting as is the locale--but only to comment that I was not truly gripped by the "unrelenting suspense" as others have been. Perhaps *Uncle Silas* is too sedate for the turbulent 20th Century (this need not apply to all 19th century books, however, witness the continued effectiveness of Mary Shelly's *Frankenstein*) or perhaps the lack of strong suspense was merely a personal failing on my part.

Irregardless, I would recommend *Uncle Silas* to those interested in the classic horror genre; historically at least it is a book that should be read. (Donna Balopole)

J(oy) P(erris) Hutton, *Too Good to Be True* (Simon, 1948; published as *The Dolphin Mystery* in 1949 by Foulsham).

The true mystery connoisseur's life is an unceasing effort to discover little known, often unreprinted, works in the genre that are invested with substantial merit.

The more fortunate among this group are able to communicate their discoveries and enthusiasm via the retrospective review section of the various magazines devoted to an appreciation of this literary field.

I am indebted to critic Robert Aucott for calling my attention to *Too Good to Be True*, and also for being kind enough to loan me his copy.

This novel bears comparison with Leigh Brackett's *No Good From a Corpse* (1944). Both novels are written by women, influenced by Chandler, and represent their creators' only essays in the hard-boiled field. (Miss Brackett did go on to write other types of mysteries. Miss Hutton's singleton is only moderately hard-boiled.)

Don Paulson isn't a private eye, but an ex-credit investigator now working in an unspecified position--mainly as a trouble shooter of the non-violent type--for Ray Menke who heads a vast industrial conglomerate in Southern California.

Paulson's interests (like those of my collaborator Marvin Lachman) are ornithological. This is admittedly an unusual hobby for the hero of the more dynamic form of the detective story to concern himself with.

Paulson is sent by Menke to help recruit an unemployed precision-instrument specialist of spectacular ability, but winds up with someone else's dead body instead. He fears that the police suspect him of complicity in this murder, and determines to investigate in spite of a warning from his boss to butt out and pay attention to business. Paulson tries to do both at the same time but somehow a few more corpses seem to keep getting in the way.

Although two decades old, this novel remains fresh and undated today. It's written with a great deal of precision, and is notable for the crystalline clarity of its plot line. It's an excellent and enjoyable novel, and well worthy of immediate revival. (Charles Shibuk)

Richard S. Prather, *Find This Woman* (Gold Medal 203, 1951; 160 pp.).

Richard S. Prather created Hollywood-based private eye Shell Scott in 1950 for Gold Medal Books when that company was just getting on its feet. The Scott novels (there are 31 so far, the last published in 1975) were tremendously popular all during the fifties and most of Gold Medal's early growth and expansion was based on the revenue from the series much as Lancer Books was built on Ted Mark's Man from Orgy and Pinnacle on Don Pendleton's Executioner.

This is Prather's and Scott's fourth time at bat and unfortunately it's one of the weaker entries in the canon.

The plot is a one line affair: Scott is in Las Vegas trying to locate a missing woman and all sorts of mobster types are out to stop him. It's more a novel of suspense than of detection; I had the "solution" figured out by page 80 without trying.

Still, Shell Scott is one of the more engaging private dicks in the genre. Six-foot-two with an inch-high snow white crewcut and a randy eye for the ladies, his adventures are a deft blend of mild sex, some smiles and fast-paced action. The guy's always pleasant company even during his more mediocre adventures, such as this one. (Stephen Mertz)

Edward Ronns (Edward S. Aarons), *State Department Murders* (Gold Medal 117, 1950, 171 pp.).

A few years back in a magazine interview Mickey Spillane cited the work of Edward S. Aarons as being worthy of attention. Since the Mick is one of my all-time favorites, that was good enough for me. But I didn't have much luck at first. Maybe I just tried the wrong books. I started a few of Aaron's Sam Durrell novels from the seventies and never made it through a one. Except for Donald Hamilton the tough guy espionage stuff generally leaves me cold, which must certainly have had something to do with my reaction. But in addition there was this peculiarity of Aarons' style that drove me nuts; his habit of describing the most minute details of a scene even during moments of action or suspense Things like stopping in the middle of a chase to relate how the trees on the far slope were bending lightly in the breeze. That sort of thing. I like my writing a bit more on the lean side.

Then I read *State Department Murders*--and I knew what Spillane was talking about.

This is a fine pulp whodunnit. The writing is smooth and compelling; always pushing forward. Aarons' eye for detailed description is present but under control. The plot is the kind of thing Hitchcock could have done wonders with: the innocent man suspected of murder, on the run from *everyone* with, naturally, an attractive but mysterious girl at his side, getting only deeper in trouble with every step he takes.

The book is also an interesting documentation of one of the darker periods of this nation's history: the McCarthy witch-hunting days. Hero Barney Cornell is an ex-OSS man facing a very McCarthy-like senate committee investigating the selling of nuclear arms secrets to the commies. Barney is innocent, of course, but that doesn't stop the Congressmen who are intent on destroying his career before a national TV audience hungry for blood.

The powerful newspaper-chain millionaire who is helping the Committee build a case against Barney--as well as against many others--is murdered. Naturally Barney is a prime suspect since in addition to having a motive he also just happened to be at the dead man's home at the time the murder occurred and (can things get any worse?) he's in love with the dead man's wife.

Considering the political climate of 1950 is probably took a lot of guts to write and publish this book since the politicians involved in the "red hunt" are cast in anything but a favorable light. In fact, in some ways in these post-Watergate times *State Department Murders* comes across as topical as any number of current Washington thrillers.

If, like me, you'd been putting off sampling Aarons, may I suggest this one as a fine place to begin. (Stephen Mertz)

THE DOCUMENTS IN THE CASE
(LETTERS)

From Larry French, 14326 Milbriar Cir., Chesterfield, MO: "The Noble Batchelors of St. Louis" will be meeting on October 8th and I have been asked to present the program dealing with John Dickson Carr's connection with Sehrlock Holmes. This particular topic is the basis of an article submitted to *Baker Street Journal* and also comprises a chapter in my book *The Grand Master of Mystery: JDC*. Carr, of course, lived in England from 1931 to 1948 and again from 1951 to 1958. In most circles he was considered an English author as opposed to American. His interest in Holmes and more specifically, his definitive biography of Conan Doyle eventually resulted in Carr being a guest of honor at the annual dinner of the "Baker Street Irregulars" in 1949. /// I received a letter from Otto Penzler today, which included a comment contribution for my *JDC Memorial Journal*. Hopefully, TMF readers have discovered Otto's "Mysterious Press" which publishes distinguished limited editions of new books by the world's greatest mystery writers. The address is Box 334, East Station, Yonkers, NY 10704. Also heard from another contributor, Joan Kahn, following her "longish vacation" on the west coast and now is trying to work her way through an "overly burdened desk". /// Please excuse the spelling of "Jeff Marle" in "The Mysterious JDC". Hopefully, readers recognized my "spoof" of Mr. Carr's middle name. I would imagine that he continually "suffered" that problem of "misinterpretation". For a short "bio" of JDC and others such as "EQ", Rex Stout and Mickey Spillane, see the now defunct *Coronet* issue of February 1956 under the entitlement of "Masters of Mystery". /// I note where Hal Knott's and Marv Lachman's listing of the "pocket books checklist" includes eight Carr books written under "Carter Dickson" and five written under "JDC". It is interesting that they published the first three books written by Carr, all featuring the French Detective, "Bencolin" (*It Walks By Night*, 1930, *Lost Gallows*, 1930 and *Castle Skull*, 1931 . . . Carr detested *Skull* and it was never published in England). Of course, "Bencolin" appeared in Carr's fourth book, *Waxworks Murder* (1932) and made his final entry in the 1937 *Four False Weapons*, being the return (ane end) of "Bencolin". /// I just finished reading Ross Macdonald's latest, *The Blue Hammer* (1976), which is mindful of a C. B. deMille epic with a "cast of thousands". I note where the Mysterious Press is coming out with a hardcover edition of Lew Archer short stories, which hopefully, should limit the number of characters and reduce the need for a "scorecard" when reading Macdonald. I concur with your review of *A Case of Spirits* and commend the Penguin series. Mike Murphy has a Vincent Starret mystery which should be selected by the Mystery Library people for reprinting. Included within the "package" is an introduction by Mike and accompanying data. How about a duplication of title: *The Corpse That Walked* (GM 1951) by Octavus Roy Cohen and *The Corpse That Walked* (Fawcett 1974) by Roy Winsor (an Edgar Award Winner). The plots, however, are totally different. /// Phil Shreffler, "Lord St. Simon", has a review of Michael Harrison's *I, Sherlock Holmes* in *Baker Street Miscellanea* No. 11. An excellent publication for "Sherlockians", subscription cost of a minimal $4 per year and can be ordered from Sciolist Press, Box 2579, Chicago, IL 60690. Jon Lellenberg is a contributing editor and does an outstanding job.

From William J. Rall, 8200 Shore Front Pkwy #5A, Rockaway Beach, NY 11693: Your current format with white pages is very easy on the eyes and the print is quite legible. /// John Dickson Carr-Carter Dickson is my all-time favorite mystery author, so I especially enjoyed Larry French's article and his letter. The Nero Wolfe Saga continues to maintain its high standard--more please. The book reviews grow better each issue. My only suggestion is to ask for more reviews of older material--mysteries that are not well known but that are still very much worth reading.

From Howard Waterhouse, Box 167, West Upton, MA 01587: It was stimulating to me to see much comment about collecting per se, (Myrtis Broset and Jeff Meyerson) in addition to such an aid to collectors as the PB check list. /// I think that the categories of collectors they describe could be expanded to great length. Jeff, there certainly are people who collect books they never read--the "completeists", who want one of each of a given category--all Pocket Books, all Avons, all Creasey or Doyle or what have you?? /// Since I collect (among other things) oddities, I'd like to hear from others who find reason to collect other than the intrinsic merit of the writer's skill. For instance, I collected and keep, Edgar Box's work, not so much for the story line as because very vew non-mystery buffs realize that "the" Gore Vidal wrote detective stories. . . . For years I collected material having to do with censorship and having taken to a work entitled *Books Fatal to Their Authors* (P. H. Ditchfield, 1895) I still am taken by books that flirt with trouble. So it's a natural for me to collect Knox who was repremanded by his ecclesiastical superiors for writing vulgar 'tec stories. (How many mystery writers also published translations of the Bible? Yes, I know at least one other, Edgar J. Goodspeed.) /// Another collect-on area that doesn't depend only upon liking the contents especially is to collect series such as the Pyramid Books "Green Door" series. Here's a limited area since only 60-70 were published which is rewarding for every one is a sterling story. A series that I've started to collect (quote them to me, friends!) is the Tired Businessman's Mystery Library. It was the series title that got me first and then the logo clinched the deal. On spine and half title is a skull with a dagger through it. Most people don't realize that on the handle of the dagger is Appleton's initial (AC) and the teeth of the skull are the series initials (TBML). Who could resist the imagination that put that package together? Besides, the authors are pretty goo also (Hume, Gregg and Grierson among others).

From Howard W. Sharpe, Box 204, St. Kilda, Vic., Australia: Last week the No. 5 (Sept.) issue of TMF reached me and reminds me that it is high time I sent a note of thanks and congratulated you on producing such a fine magazine. Not being one of the cognoscenti in the world of mystery I shall not attempt the higher flights of criticism, and in any case lack first-hand acquaintance with some of the subjects. But, taking such articles as "The Nero Wolfe Saga", "Piercing the Closed Circle (P.D. James)", "Dumbfounded in Keelerland", etc, these ring the right bell. When one is versed in the subject, they have an obvious appeal, but when one is not, then these articles stimulate one's interest and broaden one's horizon. /// As regards the many reviews, the subject of some concern and criticism, these suit me fine. At this distance from the American scene, many of the books published in your country are beyond my range normally, but if a review alerts me to a new book that seems likely to appeal to me, then I can order from a supplier in the USA. /// One thing I want to applaud is the smaller format of Nos. 4 & 5. At the reduced size they fit nicely on bookshelves and are easier to fit in.

From Frank D. McSherry, Jr., 314 W. Jackson, McAlester, OK: Re Mr. Briney's interesting letter in no. 6 (and Mr. French's) there may be another hitherto undiscovered John "Dixon" Carr story; at any rate, Bob Jones's *The Weird Menace* Index of stories of magazines in that sub-genre (published by Opar Press, 1972), lists two stories under that pen-name, the other being "The Door to Doom", from *Horror Stories* for June 1935. . . . Dunno is this is a detective story or not. . . .

From Jeff Banks, Box 3007 SFA Sta., Nacogdoches, TX 75962: I know of no higher compliment to TMF than to report honestly that I let my sub to *The Armchair Detective* expire without even noticing it for more than a couple of months. Certainly, getting what I wanted to read in TMF was the main reason for my (now corrected) oversight. /// I'm awaiting Part II of "Raymond Chandler on Flim" with 'bated breath. (Baited with what? Gin, mostly!) I'm eager to see what it will be. Screenplays for which he got credits, is my guess. Anyway, part one was a delight, and I await whatever Pete Pross has to tell us next. French on Car was (almost) equally delightful. More, please, from this fine writer! /// Also, I continue to applaud--can you hear me clapping in faraway Tennessee?--the Wolfe saga. May it be endless! If someone doesn't publish it as a book they should. /// And I've said before, I like checklists, though I know from experience they're a bitch to type. I gave my Spy Fiction students this semester a copy of the Kingsley Amis, James Bond chart from the end of *The James Bond Dossier*--hope Signet doesn't jump on me for violating copyright! And it must have taken half a dozen stencils before I managed to get it right. Then, masochist that I am, I made my own similar chart for Matt Helm adventures--any interest in publishing this? [*You bet--send it on.*] It would be a challenge to your typing ingenuity!--and probably will do one on Atlee's

(James Atlee Phillips') Joe Gall. /// Steve Lewis's "Mystery*File" reviews continue as delightful as ever. And isn't it about time you gave him a free plug for his sale of OLD RADIO tapes/casettes at decent prices and dependable quality? I think so, and am willing to offer a testimonial. I may well be his most satisfied (even if not the most frequent) customer. If you do this, be sure and print his address: Steve Lewis, 62 Chestnut Road, Newington, CT 06111. Steve is the finest you (and we) are lucky to have him! My favorite of your other reviewers--and this is a hard choice to make--is Jeff Meyerson, and I was disappointed to see so few of his reviews this time. /// I refuse to pick a favorite letter writer. After all, you know what I think of l.o.c.'s, but I have to admit that I read them. /// I like the kind of letter that asks questions, such as (1) Does anybody out there know about some of the more obscure radio shows? Who played Doc Savage (and any of his magnificent assistants) in the NYC-only radio show of the 1930s? Who played Mr. Bingler and (Carrol John Daley's) Vee Brown? (2) Can anyone tell us what authors (& in which books) made an issue of time of death of murder mystery victims? I do know that every few years one or another of the wire (news) services runs a feature story pointing out that "all those many books, movies and TV shows (I can remember when--the first time or two I saw it--they mentioned radio shows) that have the Medical Examiner (or equivalent) giving a definite time of death ("Yes, Mr. Mason, the victim died at precisely 7:22.") upon which the solution of the mystery rests are in error. Time of death just can't be determined with that great accuracy." I think they're beating the well known dead horse. But I'm still curious as to what writers in the past have made that mistake. /// Finally, I want to offer a counter-weight to George Kelley's article on Don Hamilton. I have great respect for Kelley's book reviews; I think more often than not I tend to agree with his judgments. But I disagree most strongly on the "degeneration" of Hamilton's talent. Any series hero will tend to become less convincing over the years, especially as the series passes the dozen mark. After all, there are only so many variations on derringdo--look how Edgar Rice Burroughs' bag of tricks had run down by that last Tarzan novel, over 35 years after his first. So, too, any author will have had more than enough time to state his prejudices and preferences in the first half-dozen outings for his series hero; John le Carre, Dashiell Hammett, and--if I dare mention a sacred cow--Ross Macdonald certainly did. Admittedly, so did Hamilton, and his recent comments on the auto industry, women's fashion, Women's lib, amateurs competing with professionals, callow youths and other familiar concerns have seemed repetitious over recent years. I'll even say that the comments have gotten longer as Hamilton struggled to find new ways to stress old verities. Finally, I haven't read *The Terrorizers*. Like the kindly editor, I'm getting more and more reluctant to pay full price, but I still do for the Helm and Travis McGee gooks (MacDonald is another writer recently accused of the same sort of thing) as soon as they appear locally. The latest Helm just hasn't showed up in Nacogdoches yet. /// HOWEVER, I've reread the entire Helm saga, excepting that newest book, during the past few weeks because I'm using *The Intriguers* in a Spy Fiction course. (Other writers included are Ian Fleming, Graham Greene, John le Carre, Philip Atlee, Brian Garfield, Len Deighton and William Goldman.) There has certainly been no degeneration of Hamilton's talent in recent years. Nor has the suspense gradually evaporated over the years: if Kelley thinks so, then he should look around for a writer he hasn't gotten tired of. /// I agree with him that *Line of Fire* is a very fine book. If he wants to rate it ahead of *Death of a Citizen*, I'll disagree but recognize his right to the opinion in a matter of taste. And *The Terrorizers* may not be near the top of the series—there have been one or two potboilers already, and your review seems to support the idea that this latest novel is a weak one. But the lesser Helms, usually when Hamilton leaned heaviest on Fleming's Bond books for inspiration, have often been followed by exceptionally strong ones. If *The Terrorizers* is bad, the 1979 book figures to be much better.

From Jon Breen, 10642 La Bahia Ave., Fountain Valley, CA: To begin with, I want to subscribe to volume two and will send you a check after receiving the January issue. Doesn't my one-page contribution to issue #5, by the way, entitle me to a one-issue subscription break? [*Yes, of course it does, and I'm sorry I left you off the list. I compiled the list from the tables of contents and since your contribution was not listed on the t.o.c. for #5 I overlooked it. Sorry.*] /// I don't understand David C. Ralph's complaint about Steve Lewis's reviewing. If a reviewer finds the characters boring, isn't it his province to say so? And why does such a statement represent "personal bias" any more than anything else a reviewer might say? Isn't it the reviewer's job to give a personal reaction to the book in question? And those of us who *don't* find Antony Maitland and his family boring—and in this, I would agree with Mr. Ralph—can take our differing reaction into account in deciding whether to read the book in question or not. /// While I'm sure Otto Penzler will appreciate Martin Morse Wooster's favorable review of Robert Bloch's *The King of Terrors*, I wonder if he will agree with the designation of the Mysterious Press as an "amateur press". I believe it is intended to be a professional operation in every respect, including the most important one of aiming for profit. /// I enjoy George Kelley's articles and reviews very much. His comments on Dean R. Koontz's schematic novels are to a great degree valid, but I find the Koontz novels a good deal more entertaining than Kelley's comments suggest. I also think he's too hard on Donald Hamilton—I haven't read *The Terrorizers* yet but have found most of the later Matt Helms good entertainment, though not quite up to the early ones. Still, there's nothing wrong with a reviewer being hard to please.

From Dorothy Glantz, Kloevervagen 9, S-191 47 Sollentuna, Sweden: The articles, reviews and letters of the *FANcier* kept me busy reading for many days. /// Since I received

5 numbers together, your progression from weeping and wailing over no contributions, to joy over having more than you needed was delightful. It obviously wasn't "delightful" for you, but being able to read that your frustrations eventually petered out provided this reader, at least, with a bit of underhanded chuckling. /// Contrary to some others, I rather like your personal comments in "The Nero Wolfe Saga". Your write-up has inspired me to read Stout: something which my only forage into Wolfe-land (*Please Pass the Guilt*) didn't achieve. Likewise, Art Scott's articles on HSK. For a long time I have been reading that Keeler is someone you "either love or hate". OK, says I, give him a try. *The Fourth King* was the only Keeler that the local second-hand bookstore could supply. I tired. I really did. But everything went so SLOW and I gave up. Art Scott encourages me to try again and I shall! /// Reviews by Shibuk, Lachman and Kabatchnik are always welcome and reliable. Reliable, that is, because they help me determine if I should read the book even if they didn't give it a good review. /// Since moving from the states to Sweden ten years ago, I have only spent about 3 weeks in and around New York. I don't really keep up with the English language papers and weekly magazines. In fact, my English language subscriptions are confined to the New York Times Book Review (for the sake of mainstream writing, not NC), TAD and until recently, *The MYSTERY FANcier*. But I have just received, through the *FANcier*, a crash course in women's liberation studies. Disheartened is an old-fashioned word, but it expresses my sad feelings. As editor, you have allowed some of your writers to engage in cruel below-the-belt disparagements concerning 20% of your subscribers. You're not alone. These comments pop up periodically in TAD also. But they are not quite so blatant due to, I suspect, a rather heavy use of the editorial red pencil by Al Hubin. *The FANcier* is just not the place for this discussion. I expect information and news about my crime fiction-reading hobby. I won't accept not being allowed to join in this because I am a woman. /// As one of your letter writers says, "Fandom remains about the only place a fellow can still speak his mind." Most unwillingly and very sadly, I shall leave the gentlemen to their brandy, cigars and grease guns. I do not wish to renew my subscription.
[*Huh?*]

From Susan Cramer, 3005 S. Lexington Blvd., Eau Claire, WI: Yes, I want to continue my subscription to *The Mystery Fancier*. Volume Two. Enjoy it very much--format gets better & better--digest form a real improvement. Object to Gerie Frazier's suspicions about non-working women's taste--who else has the leisure to be a mystery fanatic? Or the subsidized income to be a collector? Or the time to haunt garage sales in search of the elusive book needed to complete a series? It's allegations like hers that turn a woman to the "writings of the Women Libbers" (I agree with her "P-U").

From Bob Briney, 4 Forest Ave., Salem, MA 01970:

Some comments on Larry French's JDC article: the birth date of 30 November 1906 for Carr which I gave in my TAD "tribute" was picked up from the *New York Times* obituary, which Jeff Meyerson reprinted in *The Poisoned Pen* #2. The year 1906 was also given in the Carr entry in the *Encyclopedia of Mystery & Detection*; since this entry was based on correspondence with Carr himself, it is presumably accurate. /// The information about the "John Dixon Carr" pulp story was contained in a letter which Carr wrote in 1970 in answer to an enquiry from a fan. There is no reason to doubt this information, but there *is* reason to believe that Carr's memory of events 35 years in the past may have been incomplete. In a recent letter, Frank McSherry reminded me of Bob Jones's Index to the "weird menace" pulps, published in 1972, in which *two* "John Dixon Carr" stories are listed: "The Man Who Was Dead", *Dime Mystery*, May 1935; "The Door to Doom", *Horror Stories*, June 1935 (both published by Popular Publications, and possibly under the direction of the same editor). Together with the story which Mike Nevins mentioned--"Terror's Dark Tower", *Detective Tales*, October 1935--this makes at least three pulp stories by Carr. Copies of these three magazines must be in the hands of pulp collectors. It would be nice to rescue these stories from their present obscurity, even if they turn out to be lesser efforts or versions of plots that Carr re-used later. /// The mystery novels of John Holbrook Vance (full name of sf writer Jack Vance) have from time to time been mentioned approvingly in the mystery press: *The Man in the Cage*, *The Fox Valley Murders*, *Bad Ronald*, etc. It was quite a shock to receive a recent catalogue (#12) of Vance manuscripts from small-pressman and bookseller Roy Squires, and to note that the offerings included the manuscripts of two *unpublished* Vance novels, *The Dark Ocean* and *Strange People, Queer Notions*. Squires says, "That the two completed novels . . . remain unpublished is beyond my ability to explain. [They are] exceptionally entertaining . . . tightly plotted and well told." Publishers, get on the ball!

From Jim Goodrich, 5 Ulster Road, New Paltz, NY 12561: [. . .] Helen and I were enjoying the Bouchercon in the wilds of Manhattan. Chris & Otto put on a fine show at the posh Waldorf. In between events we met Steve Lewis, Jack (Pulps) Irwin & Mary Ann Grochowski (Suspense Unltd.) plus I renewed acquaintances with Charlie Shibuk & Marv Lachman. All wonderful people, even divorced from detective matters. /// Re Pross' Chandler film checklist, the infamous Raymond Rohauer once mentioned that *Murder My Sweet* had an underground rep for being tainted by Commie influence, in that the producer, director & writer were on the black list of the McCarthy era. *The Big Sleep* may have been officially released 8/31/46 but I saw it in the army at least 2 months earlier. [. . .] /// Had mixed feelings when I read the glowing reviews of *The Man With Bogart's Face* in TMF #3. The author, Andy Fenady, went to college with me in Toledo, Ohio. At that time he was a very talented but egotistical theatre major. We both went to H'wood about the same time, in the early 50's; I gave up any ideas of making it in show

biz, while A. J. stayed on to make films. Now I'm a college librarian & he is branching out into novels. Snif, snif. /// Forgot to mention that I also met Jeff Meyerson at the Bouchercon. Next year perhaps you & I will encounter one another at the Pulpcon in St. Louis!
[*I don't know about the Pulpcon, but I'm going to next year's Bouchercon if I have to walk all the way to Chicago.*]

From Dorothy Juri, 175 Pineview Lane, Menlo Park, CA 94025: I would like to pursue Gerie Fraziers' comment on women mystery readers. I can only speak from my own experience. When I was old enough to go to the Public Library, I fell under the spell of Augusta Huill Seamon, a writer of children mysteries. I was hooked for all time. I then progressed to Doyle, Sax Rohmer etc. Mysteries thrilled and scared me. Yes scared, believe it or not in this day of television, where there is no mystery allowed, or the imagination stimulated, I was frightened by *The Green Eyes of Bast* by Rohmer for one. Later on, I read Van Dine's *Greene Murder Case* until two in the morning and stayed awake the rest of the night with the light on. That story was my first touch with a vicious insanity. On looking back on some of Van Dine's books, there seems to be a touch of the grotesque in some, not usually connected with Philo Vance, the sophisticate. /// I have tried to interest my children in the mystery story, but have succeeded with only one out of five. He was thoroughly hooked on reading Arthur Upfield's *The Mountains Have a Secret*, and is now as bad as I am. I envy all that he has before him in discovering all that I have behind me. /// I would like to know just ouw others of your women subscribers became interested in the mystery, interested enough to seek out publications such as yours. /// As a note, I thought for many years John Rhode was a pseudonym for John Dickson Carr, mainly because the small brance library where I lived had indicated so.

From Peter Pross, 1303 Willis St., Richmond, VA 23224: George Kelley's short piece regarding Donald Hamilton was enjoyable; I'll take George's word and stay clear of Hamilton's recent books. Kelley's and Jane Bakerman"s reviews are perceptive and informative. Also, the Nero Wolfe Saga is, I believe, improving with every issue. Finally, Myrtis Broset's comment on mystery collectors rings a bell. I have often wondered in which direction I would run (toward my Chandler's or my wife) if my house caught on fire. I guess the only solution is to flip a coin or take out fire insurance.

From James A. Jobst, 2451 S. Gaylord #3, Denver, CO 80210: Let me first tell you how much I enjoy receiving *The Mystery Fancier* every other month. It certainly fills the gaps that *The Armchair Detective* doesn't fill. I particularly enjoy the reviews of the old books. I have just started collecting myself, even though I have read mystery and detective fiction for about ten years. My budget can't afford the first editions, but I am into the paperbacks of the 40's and 50's. I wonder if there are others out there who are doing the same thing I am. The "Checklists" that appeared in issues 2, 3 and 6 were particularly helpful to me. It gives me a good feeling to walk into a used bookstore and actually find an old Dell "Map Back" mystery, especially if it is in good condition. I am sure that some of the mysteries that I have in my collection have been sitting up in somebody's attic for the last 20 or 30 years. /// I was glad to see that Donald E. Westlake is finally getting the praise he finally deserves. I remember taking his books out of the library before they were being issued in paperback. I enjoy writers with a sense of humor. /// With the rise in popularity of Arthur W. Upfield, is any publishing company reissueing any of the Bonaparte mysteries? In 1963 and 64 Berlkey Medallion came out with six of his titles, but I haven't seen anything since by an American publishing company. Pan Books of London came out with about a dozen in the early 70's, but they are awfully hard to come by around Denver. /// Please keep up the good work and I hope the circulation increases in 1978. Your Nero Wolfe Saga is delightful and thanks to Art Scott (#2) for his review of Chip Harrison's (Lawrence Block) *Make Out With Murder* and *The Topless Tulip Caper*. I haven't been able to find the former, but the latter was very good. I enjoy pastiches and I think Rex Stout would have enjoyed them too.

From Ilse Goldsmith, Park Court, Middletown, NY 10940: I personally am delighted with the paperback size of the fanzine, because TMF tucks so neatly into pocket or purse. I travel by car a great deal in the course of my day's work, and my reading material must be small enough to be handy. Now TMF is my seat-side as well as my bed-side companion! /// I have been enjoying TMF's last issues more than the recent issues of TAD. Today's TAD seems weightier and more text-like than earlier issues. I have many times been frustrated when reading TAD because my background reading knowledge is so much poorer than most of its readers, but I enjoyed TAD's light touch and envied the "contributory clique" their wealth of information and camaraderie---so please keep up the delightful work and lighter touch of TMF. /// I am taking umbrage with Geri Frazier's comments on women subscribers and readers---ones sex does *not* determine ones interests!!!!!!! or lack of interests!! Many women not working are serious readers--as are many men. The difference between subscribers may be lack of knowledge about a magazine--Women working (and not working) have a drawback. They do not have the "old boy" network and perhaps that is why female mystery addicts do not know each other. But please, Ms. Frazier, play fair. Intelligence and good taste are not sex linked characteristics! [. . .] /// I enjoyed Mr. French's article on John Dickson Carr and am looking forward to his JDC Memorial. I was not aware that Mr. Carr's signatures are so rare. He is one of my favorite authors, and I have a personal letter from him which I cherish (I sent a photocopy of that letter and signature to Mr. French). Mr. Carr's passing saddened us all, and he will be sorely missed. /// One more query--is there a Michael Gilbert checklist available? Most book lists do not contain his books, and I need a checklist to inquire about him.

From Myrtis Broset, 204 S. Spalding St., Spring Valley, IL: Back in April there was an article in the New York *Times*, wherein the statement was made that "readers prefer violent action to deliberate ratiocination, there's little demand for the novel in which a policeman carefully sorts and tracks down clues to reach a solution." /// Again on October 2nd in the column "Paperback Talk" Ray Walter says "Apart from Agatha Christie, how is the crime novel doing these days? Many publishers, when the question is raised, murmur that it isn't what it once was." Joan Kahn of Harper and Row believes "that the bottom was plumbed in the mid 60's." /// Yet the same column states that according to a Gallup poll, 53% of all college readers are avid readers of crime stories, and there is a continuing, steady demand for the work of such old-timers as Rex Stout, Ellery Queen, Erle Stanley Gardner, Mickey Spillane, John D. MacDonald and Ross Macdonald. /// Evidently the reason more mystery books are not published is because the publishers believe there is no demand for them. Where do they get this idea? Is it that readers do not want mysteries or is it that they just can't find them?

From Gerie Frazier, 280 River Road, 98-A, Piscataway, NJ: I HATE Mondays, but September 19th was greatly improved by the arrival of TMF. Answering comments of Jeff Meyerson and Myrtis Broset: yes, indeed--Guy [*Guy Frazier, that is--ed.*] and I are collecting ALL Nero Wolfe stories, mostly not previously read. Also books by Louis L'Amour (Westerns) unread. Got "hooked" on those temporarily--not abandoning mysteries. /// Hope y'all will bear with my early letters; am afflicted by a malady I call "Nero Wolfe mania" and because of Guy Townsend's Saga and interest shown by others, want to pass on information. /// We bought *Corsage* (Michael Bourne, editor) and learned from it that two movies were "adapted" from Stout's Nero Wolfe novels. In 1936, *Fer-de-Lance* was filmed as *Meet Nero Wolfe* with Edward Arnold as Wolfe, Lionel Stander as Archie. In 1937 *The League of Frightened Men* was filmed with Walter Connally as Wolfe, Lionel Stander as Archie. Rex Stout wanted Charles Laughton to play Wolfe, but Laughton was not available at the time. In the 1940's Sydney Greenstreet played Wolfe in a "thoroughly unfaithful radio series" according to Mr. Bourne. In late 1960's a NW TV series was produced in Italy. /// Wrote to Editor of TV Mailbag in the Kansas City *Star* regarding a possible TV series and he replied: "ABC has a made-for-TV movie cooking, *Nero Wolfe*, based on one of Rex Stout's classic stories about the legendary detective. Thayer David will star in the movie, which is promised for sometime this season." Wolfe fans be on the look-out for that. /// Any devotees of Rex Stout and/or Nero Wolfe should be pleased to read (or own) *Corsage*. It contains, in full, "Bitter End", previously printed only in *The American Magazine*; an interesting interview of Stout by Bourne, and a complete (hopefully) list of the Nero Wolfe stories. /// Many thanks to Peter

Pross for "Raymond Chandler on Film"--an enjoyable trip down memory lane!!

From E. F. Bleiler, Dover Publications, 180 Varick St, NY NY: If I can make one unasked-for criticism: your earlier format was much preferable to the present. The larger pages not only looked neater, but were easier to read. [. . .] /// The Mystery Library keeps expanding, not as fast as I would like, but some. We have just published:
- Collins, Wilkie--*Little Novels*. About half the stories in it are mystery or detection. Never before published in the USA.
- Van Gulik--*The Haunted Monastery, The Chinese Maze Murders*. Two novels in one volume.
- Leblanc--*The Exploits of Arsene Lupin*. The first series.
- Rohmer--*The Dream Detective*.
- Wood--*The Passenger from Scotland Yard*. Victorian detective novel.

This is our schedule for the near future:
- Stribling--*Clues of the Caribees*, October 1977.
- King, C. Daly--*The Curious Mr. Tarrant*, October 1977.
- LeFanu--*Wylder's Hand*, February 1978.
- Oppenheim--*The Great Impersonation*, February 1978.
- Collins, Wilkie--*No Name*, April 1978.
- White, T. H.--*Darkness at Pemberley* (The *Sword and the Stone* man), April 1978.
- Vickers--*The Department of Dead Ends*, April 1978. A new selection.
- Bleiler, ed.--*Three Victorian Detective Novels*. The *Unknown Weapon*, Forrester, from *The Female Detective* (1864); *My Lady's Money*, Wilkie Collins; *The Big Bow Mystery*, Zangwill. May 1978.
- Thomson--*Masters of Mystery*. With corrections. May 1978.

Further titles, in the works but not yet definitely scheduled, are *Best Old Man in the Corner Stories*, Baroness Orczy; *The Triumphs of Eugene Valmont*, Robert Barr; *Exploits of Fidelity Dove*, Vickers; *Best Supernatural Stories of A. Conan Doyle*; *Loveday Brooke*, Mrs. Pirkis; and perhaps *Thrilling Stories of the Railroad*, Whitechurch. /// On the last item, we are curious to see what will happen to books that are primarily collectors' items, on the general market. The response to *The Curious Mr. Tarrant* will give us some indication.

www.ingramcontent.com/pod-product-compliance
Lightning Source LLC
Chambersburg PA
CBHW031428040426
42444CB00006B/733